Preaching Today

DECLARING THE FAITH

Preaching Today

D. W. CLEVERLEY FORD

EPWORTH PRESS & SPCK

251
F751

179724

© D. W. Cleverley Ford
First published in 1969 by
Epworth Press and SPCK
Printed in Great Britain by
Cox & Wyman Limited
London, Fakenham and Reading

SBN 7162 0125 9 (Epworth)
SBN 281 02342 5 (SPCK)

Contents

Preface   vii

Prologue – The Pulpit   ix

1. Objections to Preaching   1

2. The Origins of Preaching   19

3. The Content of Preaching   33

4. The Form of Preaching   47

5. The Place of Preaching   65

6. The Future of Preaching   79

Epilogue – Preaching in Context   107

Acknowledgements

The author is grateful to the following for permission to include in this book extracts from other works: Mrs J. F. Andrews (P. T. Forsyth, *Positive Preaching and the Modern Mind*, Independent Press); Faber and Faber Ltd (*The Letters of Ezra Pound*, quoted by Herbert Read in *The True Voice of Feeling*); Hodder and Stoughton Ltd (Paul Scherer, *The Word God Sent*); S.C.M. Press Ltd (J. C. Hoekendijk, *The Church Inside Out*; Alan Richardson, *Preface to Bible Study*; R. E. C. Browne, *The Ministry of the Word*; Albert van den Heuvel, *The Humiliation of the Church*). Quotations from the Bible are from the *Revised Version* of 1881 unless otherwise stated. Quotations from the *New English Bible*, copyright 1961, are included by permission of the Oxford and Cambridge University Presses.

Preface

THIS book has been written in response to an invitation from the Reverend Michael Perry, Chief Assistant for Home Publishing of the S.P.C.K. It owes much to a group which meets half-yearly to discuss problems connected with present-day preaching. The membership consists of the Reverends Canon Max Warren, D.D., Canon Bryan S. W. Green, D.D., Professor Anthony Hanson, D.D., Canon Michael Stancliffe, Canon Joseph Robinson, Mark Gibbard, S.S.J.E., and E. M. B. Green. While, however, I am greatly indebted to the group for the stimulus provided by its lively debate, it cannot be held responsible for any of the statements made in this book. For these I must be held to account. I am grateful for some suggestions of Michael Perry about the form of my manuscript, to the Reverend Gordon S. Wakefield and the Editorial Department of the Epworth Press for some improvements which they recommended, and to Mrs J. Hodgson for preparing the typescript and correcting the proofs.

Kensington 1969   D. W. CLEVERLEY FORD

Prologue

The Pulpit

Lord, I am afraid of my pulpit.
> I am afraid it is irrelevant.
> I am afraid of the demands it makes upon
> > my time and energy.
And yet it stands there in the Church.
> It stands to tell me I must speak.
> It stands to speak as once it spoke to me.
> So I must mount its steps again.

> But what shall I say?
> And how shall I say it?
> And who will listen?
> And who will benefit?

> Speaking is a serious business.
> Speaking tells the man you are.
> Speaking makes the Church that is.
> And speaking can betray.

Lord, I am afraid of my pulpit.
      Thy pulpit,
      The Church's pulpit.
I am afraid that the things the Church is saying by
its clumsy, awkward, slow administration counteract
the message of its Christ.
      And is it Christlike?
      Is it humble?
How often does it stoop to wash another's feet?

Lord, I am afraid of my pulpit.
      Because I am a member of the Church.
      Because I am a sinner with the Church.
      And I partake of all her faults.

And yet I have to preach.
      I have to preach before the Sacrament.
      I have to preach where men can answer back
      in groups, discussion and in dialogue.

Lord, I am afraid of my pulpit.
      Give me grace to see its relevance.
      Give me grace to trust its future.
      Give me words to speak Thy grace.
      Thy grace which called
      Thy grace which equipped
      Thy grace which I encountered
      through the words our Saviour uttered;
      Probing words,
      Cleaning words,
      Healing words.
      The words of the Word made flesh, spoken
      from the pulpit of his body,
      Jesus Christ our Lord.

Preaching Today

1. Objections to Preaching

PREACHING has a strange quality about it. As commonly understood, one part of us hates it. We hate being 'preached at', and if someone is foolish enough to make the attempt in a private conversation we go off 'in a huff'. And yet we expect preaching in a church. The layman expects it. He even reckons he has been cheated if he does not get it. He likes to be stirred, argued with, and even shaken. Writing the leading article in that fashionable glossy magazine *Queen*, a journalist told of his search in London for a preacher 'who would twist you savagely out of your seat with sheer oratory, fill you with bubbling enthusiasm and send you out with one good purpose to live and die for.' And the year? 1963, not 1863. Three years later a young Anglican clergyman was surprised that a BBC newsman was ready to travel fifty miles in order to collect a five-minute comment on a preaching conference. 'Oh, but,' came the reply, 'the British public is always interested in preaching.'

Is this true? Does the average man with any leanings towards church-going, however occasionally, really count preaching as high among the Church's chief activities? If so, is he wrong? Is he merely old-fashioned? It is true, of course, that the sermon has a great and honourable history in England. For three centuries, from the Elizabethans to the Victorians, the sermon in published form might well be a 'best seller',[1] but in the twentieth century it scarcely sells at all. Was the Church, therefore, unenlightened for three centuries to pay such attention to the pulpit? Or is it that preaching is an *inappropriate* tool for the present?

Probably there exists a general reluctance to pronounce a final verdict. All that will be said is that preaching seems to be out of tune with the times. It doesn't fit the nineteen-seventies. Technological man has no ears for it. These opinions are what constitute the modern objection to preaching, and it stems not so much from foes outside the Church as from friends within it. Thus Canon John V. Taylor writes, 'But the old unquestioned monologue of the pulpit is less appropriate to our searching and tentative age than the interchange of discussion. More and more we ought to expect group study and exploration to do in our own day what sermons have done in the past.'[2]

Perhaps, therefore, we might assert (but it is only part of the truth) that what is inappropriate about preaching is its form. Preaching *as a method* is outdated. It is no longer a suitable instrument for the Church's witness. The content, of course, always is relevant. It is an eternal Gospel Christianity has to proclaim, but the method of proclamation has changed because the world has changed. Albert van den Heuvel quotes Karl Barth as saying, 'Our preaching does not differ in essence from that of the prophets and apostles who "saw and touched"; the difference is due to the different historical setting in which it takes place.'[3] 'Some difference!' comments van den Heuvel. 'That is exactly what the whole struggle in the Church is about: the only difference is the historical setting!'[4] As Per Lönning has pointed out, the struggle between orthodoxy and heterodoxy as represented by 'The Enlightenment', 'Liberal Protestantism', and the 'New Theology' consists in the dilemma

---

[1] See Arthur Pollard, *English Sermons*; Longmans Green, 1963.
[2] C.M.S. News Letter N. 310, November 1967.
[3] *Prayer and Preaching*; S.C.M. Press, p. 68.
[4] *The Humiliation of the Church*; S.C.M. Press, 1967, p. 68.

of having to proclaim an unchanging Gospel in a changing world.[1]

Our first approach, therefore, is to examine some of the features of the *contemporary historical setting* in order to see what makes preaching objectionable as a method for the conduct of the Church's mission today.

First, this is *an age of questioning*. More than that, it is an age which insists on asking its own questions; that is to say, what is demanded is not only the liberty of free inquiry, but the liberty of independent inquiry. Not only must some men be allowed to question anything, but all men must be allowed to question everything – and everybody. What we see is questioning added to independence, a mood which had its first strong stirrings in the Europe of 1848. Since then people have been less and less willing to submit to government unless having a say in government. And nowadays even student bodies call for a voice in shaping their curricula.

Obviously this mood of independent inquiry militates against preaching. It militates against it because preaching involves the exercise of authority. What is meant is not only the apparent authority which the traditional exercise of preaching presents – a pulpit, distinctive clothing, and a licence to preach – but the authority which is implicit in preaching itself. But is that authority justified? This is the modern question. And wherein does the authority reside? In the message? In the tradition? In the preacher himself? What we cannot do is bypass authority in preaching.[2] It is this element, among others, that raises the objections to preaching on the part of modern man.

Preaching also appears to be an authority which gives answers. Not simply answers to questions no one is asking (nothing serves to make preaching more irrelevant than this) but answers when what is felt to be the overriding need is more questions.

[1] *The Dilemma of Contemporary Theology*; Universitetsforlaget Oslo, 1962, p. 120.

[2] For an elaboration of this see John Bright, *The Authority of the Old Testament*; S.C.M. Press, 1967, p. 21.

Apparently the Divinity Faculty of the University of Cambridge was sufficiently aware of this modern need in 1963, for instead of advertising its public lectures as explanations of Christian doctrine after the manner of J. S. Whale in 1940, it called them instead *Objections to Christian Belief*,[1] and so won a hearing. And what is more significant, when the Humanists followed, they did not fall back on their traditional line of attacking the established Churches, they wrote a book called *Objections to Humanism*.[2] By 1963 the point had been grasped that if a preacher wishes to be heard by the men of his time, it is teasing questions he must provide, not neat answers.

But is this possible? Preaching, according to the New Testament, is essentially proclamation. It is proclamation of Christ. Is this something which is *able* to be presented in the form of questions? Perhaps it is on the discovery of new techniques at this point that the appropriateness of preaching as a tool for the mission of the Church in the mid-twentieth century will ultimately depend. If so, it will not be the first time in its long history that preaching has had to adapt itself to the prevailing thought-forms of the age in which it is exercised, and so has survived.

A *second* feature of the contemporary scene is the *stress on team-work*. Modern man does not himself carry through the whole project on which he is engaged. This is true not only of the operative in a large motor-car works, but of the research chemist working in a laboratory to discover the causes of cancer. And more and more even the medical practitioner, including the General Practitioner, works as a member of a small team, and in close conjunction with biological chemists in a laboratory. And the head of an industrial department, even the Managing Director of the complete organization, does not operate as an individual, but as the 'king-pin' in a network of co-workers. Modern technological enterprise is too complicated to be carried through from start to finish by one man. Today a worker's

[1] Published by Constable, 1963.
[2] Constable, 1963, now in paperback; Pelican Books, 1965.

4

responsibilities belong to the carrying out of one part of a section of a complete project.

This use of a team, which is clearly necessitated by the magnitude of modern production, is also a feature of modern means of communication. Here its necessity is not so obvious. Nowadays, however, it is not one speaker who appears on television to describe, for example, the latest strike situation, but a group of three men sitting round a table questioned by a fourth. The effect of this method is not the handing out of information by some superior person who knows all the answers, which the hearers must either take or leave. The listener, who is also the viewer, makes up his own mind about what is happening from the various opinions expressed by the various speakers in answer to the questions that are asked. The method amounts to a reduction of the element of authority in the communication of information. The hearer makes up his own mind by overhearing a team of experts discussing. His conclusions may not be those of any of the team, but they are his own, and they have not been imposed on him from above.

The same method operates more and more in modern educational methods in schools. Teaching is so devised that what the pupils are provided with is not so much a set of answers as a set of key questions to which they themselves must find the answers. So they are taught initiative and the capacity to play a part in co-operative enterprises. At the university level more use is made of the seminar than of the lecture, and in all adult education it is on the discussion group that most weight is placed for, as Symanowski writes, 'In a circle everyone has the same right: no one is elevated above the rest. Everyone has the same chance if he opens his mouth. The one who puts the brakes on the conversation by his contradictions helps to achieve an even greater depth and clarity.'[1]

In contradistinction from this modern approach through team work, preaching appears as solo work, and as such is

[1] Horst Symanowski, *The Christian Witness in an Industrial Society*; Collins, 1966.

5

outdated. Not only is its delivery a monologue but its preparation is carried out by the preacher alone in his study, and the end product is the result of his own labour, capacity and experience. The method is objectionable because it suggests both superiority and narrowness on the part of the preacher, the two together making it worse. Unless preaching can adapt itself to the modern predilection for co-operative team work, thus reducing its authoritative aspect, or is able to show that it is something which can stand in its own right because of its special nature – that is to say, unless preaching is demonstrably *sui generis* – it must fail to commend itself to modern man.

A *third* feature is the modern use of *the visual image*, though the visual image is not itself modern. Since the dawn of history there have been artists and sculptors. Judaism stood out as the exception among the religions because the likeness of anything in heaven or on earth was not permitted. Man has always responded to visual images. What we see, however, in the modern world is an enormous advance in the richness and variety of the visual image captivating the mind of modern man. The line of development has been from the camera producing black and white still pictures to the coloured sound motion picture televised and even recorded for reproduction. Coupled with this has been an enormous advance in colour printing and lithographic processes so that national newspapers produce their coloured week-end supplements mainly of reproduced coloured photographs. Scarcely any printing matter is circulated without its accompanying pictures. Company Reports bear the aspect of glossy magazines. Line drawings also, even cartoons, figure now in what used to be, and still is to some extent, prosaic printed matter. Strip, diagrams, and symbols are visual aids in widespread use. Add to this the use of the film and television to entertain and provide information, with drama looked upon as a more effective way of holding up a mirror to contemporary society than the sermon, and it is not difficult to see how the spoken word without visual aids, the speaker's stock-in-trade, is objected to as inappropriate in this modern, picture-conditioned age.

The objection has an even sharper point, since the Church, in deference to a scientific age, has turned to presenting its message more in terms of an abstraction, the most notable example of which is the phrase 'the Ground of our Being'.

Demythologizing of the scriptures has also acted as an image-stripping process resulting in preaching bereft of the biblical word pictures which down the ages have played no small a part in the success of the preacher's art of communication.

A *fourth* characteristic of the age which has a bearing on preaching is *speed*. Speed is too obvious a feature of modern life to need stressing. Suffice it to say that a news item in *The Times* of 4th October 1967 reported that Major William Knight of the U.S. Air Force set up a new speed record of 4,534 m.p.h. (that is, seven times the speed of sound) using the experimental X–15 rocket aircraft. Because of the general hurry of modern living there is more and more a reliance on the News Headlines, the Caption, the Summary of Today's Events, and the 'Digest' of various publications in the Sunday newspapers. Moreover, the size of the flood of printed material in the form of magazines, journals, periodicals, reports, 'White Papers', memoranda, quarterlies, and monthlies, not to mention books, hard-back and paperback, has driven the weighed-down reader to evolve, if possible, speed in reading. Speed-writing has now been followed by speed-reading. There are speed-records in this field to be won, so many words per minute; and progress in velocity is measurable week by week. Furthermore, in order to save yet more time, the whole process of listening, writing, and reading is being short cut by the extended use of the tape-recorder. Not even the student, if he is up to date, carries a notebook any longer, and certainly not the reporter. He uses 'tape' and hears it played back. He does not write and read. He is saving time. For such a modern man to sit listening to an argument developed

in a sermon is like inviting him to ride in a barouche, an experience novel and even fascinating, but outside his everyday world
of hard realities where decisions have to be made precisely and
with speed. Unless preaching can assist hurrying men in a
speedy world, the objection will be sustained that it has no
ustifiable existence except as a museum piece.

So much for the *form* of preaching, that is, the traditional
sermon in monologue. Supposing, however, it can be modern-
ized, supposing it can be shaped to gear into modern man's
questing mind, suppose the preacher can appear as the spokes-
man of a team, suppose he can appeal to man's need of graphic
images and keep pace with his hurrying footsteps – are we sure
that the *content* of preaching is not also inappropriate to modern
man? Let us look at some of the chief features of his life.

First, the *prevailing preoccupation with the secular*. This is not
to charge the age in which we live with having succumbed to
secularism, but to observe that modern life is lived not only
apart from ecclesiastical control, but apart from metaphysical
considerations. At the popular level this exhibits itself in a
general preoccupation with the material benefits and gadgets of
technological progress, and they undoubtedly provide a satisfaction within a limited, even if extensive, field of human
experience, not to be despised. This situation, for general purposes, might be described as a widespread materialism in Western
nations. At the more reflective levels of society it means an
interest in the functional with a consequent by-passing of the
metaphysical. It is not that the latter is so much denied as left
out of account. There is so much of absorbing interest in manipu-
lating the resources of nature for ends chosen by man, and so
many rewards for exercising human skill and ingenuity in this
field, that it is not apparent what comparable obvious and
immediate benefits can accrue from a consideration of the
metaphysical. The word 'functional' is a key word of the age.
This can be seen in modern architecture, for the architecture of
a period is frequently the embodiment of its prevailing spirit;

8

and in the mid-twentieth century, buildings are not primarily designed for their appearance, or to convey an idea, but for the function they are intended to perform. It is an approach as opposed as it could be to that which lay behind the designing of Temple Meads Station in Bristol and St Pancras Station in London.

In recent years this life of society in the secular has been the subject of extensive theorizing, notably by van Peursen who sees a line of development in the thinking of mankind from the mythological to the ontological (or metaphysical), and now on to the functional. Arend Th. van Leewen sees two eras, the ontocratic and the technocratic. More widely read than either of these Dutch writers is the American, Harvey Cox, author of *The Secular City*.[1] He separates out three stages which roughly correspond to van Peursen's analysis; the tribe, the town, and now the city. It is city dwelling that is characteristic of the present period of history; the secular city, technopolis with its twin features of anonymity and mobility. This is modern man's address. It is here that he 'lives, moves and has his being', and metaphysics has no part to play in the scaffolding of his thinking.

Manifestly this is not a situation – if the above is a true description of our times – in which the pulpit as traditionally used has any obvious part to play. The objection against it is that it lies outside the sphere of men's current interests. It is like a seaport, once useful, but from which the tide of human affairs has receded, leaving it high and dry. And so the task some modern theologians have engaged in is to inquire if the dried-out port can once more be connected with the sea. The result has been what can be called the Secular Theologies, the extreme position on the left being occupied by van Buren, and the more moderate position by the late Ronald Gregor Smith and Bishop John Robinson. The question for us to ask is, 'Are these secular theologies capable of giving the pulpit relevance in an age pre-occupied with the functional?' Harvey Cox is certain that they

[1] S.C.M. Press, 1965.

9

can,[1] and has much to say about preaching. For him, preaching is the proclamation of what God is doing in the secular.[2] This certainly might be called prophecy, but does it measure up to the place St Paul accorded in his preaching to Christ crucified? The cross does not figure largely in Harvey Cox's book. Maybe, however, the important question to ask in the light of all the secular theologies is, 'What is there to proclaim without the transcendent?' The modern insights concerning the secular undoubtedly point to a truth; and as Charles Davis has shown in his book *God's Grace in History*,[3] the secular by no means dispenses with the sacred, but a battle for preaching will have to be fought on the grounds of the transcendent unless the assumption can be made that Humanism with a difference (what Thomas Keir in *The Word in Worship*[4] calls 'Humanism in a Cassock') is sufficient to sustain preaching in the modern world.

A *second* feature of modern life which would seem to relegate the pulpit to the museum is the *modern lordship of science*. As W. Macneile Dixon expressed it in his Gifford lectures as long ago as 1935–37, the situation used to be *Roma locuta causa finita est*; now, however, it is *Scientia locuta causa finita est*.[5] 'Science has spoken, the matter is ended.' It is true, of course, that the lordship of science[6] has not gone without challenge.

---

[1] 'We must learn, as Bonhoeffer said, to speak of God in a secular fashion and find a non-religious interpretation of biblical concepts. It will do no good to cling to our religious and metaphysical versions of Christianity in the hope that one day religion or metaphysics will once again be back. They are disappearing for ever and that means we can now let go and immerse ourselves in the new world of the secular city.' *The Secular City*, p. 4.

[2] Ibid., p. 122. The general weakness of approaches of this kind is a lack of awareness of the fundamental contradiction in the nature of man.

[3] Collins (Fontana), 1966.

[4] Oxford University Press, 1962.

[5] *The Human Situation*; Pelican, 1958.

[6] For a recent statement of the authoritative position science has won, see David Jenkins, *Guide to the Debate about God*; Lutterworth Press, 1966, pp. 13–18.

Aldous Huxley wrote, chiefly in his *Brave New World*, as an iconoclast of the achievements of science, sociology, and psychology, debunking scientific utopianism. D. H. Lawrence, too, inveighed in his own way against the threat to humanity and persons latent in modern scientifically-determined society. Generally speaking, however, it is popularly thought that science has the answers, though there may be signs at the moment of a swing from science to the arts, and the escape into the fantasy world of drugs may not be without significance.

In the presence of the popular lordship of science the objection to preaching is that it is unscientific. What this in fact implies is that in so far as reason occupies a place in it, it is deductive reasoning and not inductive. Moreover, the propositions which it asserts are not subject to verification by experiment. Readiness to experiment is one of the scientific approaches that has caught hold widely among modern youth. Anything may be tried. Preaching, therefore, is at a discount because no small part of what it proclaims is not subject to experiment. It is not possible to try out the doctrine of the resurrection. Moreover, this impossibility of experimentation is confused with an unwillingness for experimentation. And so the pulpit is objected to as completely out of alignment with the spirit of the age.

Furthermore, the modern scientific spirit runs counter not only to the content of preaching, but in some respects to the form which preaching of necessity takes. Preaching requires personal involvement not only on the part of those to whom the sermon is addressed, but on the part of the preacher. Preaching is truth through personality. It is the Word become flesh. The scientific method, however, is careful not to let personality obtrude. It is detached. Science, of course, is aware that this is impossible of complete achievement. The observer affects what he observes. And from another aspect, the disciplines of science require a high degree of personal dedication, without which no results are obtained. Nevertheless, in a general way, to study a question scientifically does mean to study it unemotionally, that is, without allowing the feelings of the person to prejudice the issue. Science, then, requires personal detachment. Preaching, however, requires personal involvement. This in turn affects speaking. A scientist, to be convincing, must address his audience unemotionally, if not in a 'dead-pan' voice. Any rhetorical effects, passion, or emotional pressure would at once arouse suspicion. But in the case of the preacher, the situation is otherwise. As Peter Brown has written in his book *Augustine of Hippo*, 'An audience will identify itself only with an excited man: and Augustine would be excited for them.'[1]

Does the lordship of science mean the final demise of preaching, its content and its form, as being unscientific? Or does the protest of existentialism offer an alternative approach to reality and so provide a justification of preaching? This is the context in which the objection to preaching as unscientific needs to be considered.

A *third* feature of modern life is *the relegation of the activity of the Church to the margin of society*.

This is a new situation. The Church has in the past been a pillar, if not the cement, of Western civilization. And church-going was compulsory. In Elizabethan times the compulsion centred upon a monetary fine for absence. In Victorian times the compulsion was both the necessity for a mark of respectability, and the need to occupy the time throughout a dull Sunday. Manifestly, then, skilled preachers were popular. They at least relieved the tedium. They could even be exciting. People queued up for their favourites. Picture postcards were sold of some as film stars of today. The only slight parallel that still exists to this bygone situation is in those few places where the church parade service still obtains. Then the 'star preacher' is a benediction.

But what when the only compulsion for church-going is the internal one that already exists in the hearts of the faithful? What when the Church has all but lost its status and its establishment and what there is, is counted in some quarters as a hindrance? What when the man who attends church is reckoned

[1] Faber and Faber, 1967, p. 252.

12

as an anomaly in society? Will preaching rank as high in importance under such modern conditions? It is true the small modern congregation of the faithful will be grateful for the stimulating preacher, but they will count him as a luxury they cannot demand or even expect. And they will still assemble even if he is absent. Under these conditions the demand for preaching is diminished; and when the demand diminishes, so does the supply. And when both are down, how undernourished will the Church become with a bread and water diet?

It may be that the Church's loss of status is an advantage. It may be that relegation to the margin of society offers an opportunity for repentance of the petty pomposity of parsons which has bedevilled too many too long. It may be that there is offered the chance of a new beginning; a willingness to assume authority only when it is freely bestowed by a discerning and grateful public; a readiness to begin at the lowest level, a place close to that occupied by Jesus who worked with no more status at the outset than a manger for a cradle, a provincial town for a university, and carpentry for a profession. Perhaps the clergyman will take to re-thinking what he really is, for at the moment he is lacking self-assurance.[1] But with regard to these things, the objector must be forgiven if he says, 'The time is not yet!' So far he does not see renewal in banishment to the margin; he sees only banishment, and, so he thinks, deserved.

There are others who perceive *no* hope of renewal on the part of the structured Church. 'Almost without exception,' writes J. C. Hoekendijk, 'the Churches in Western Europe still function only in a part of the classical milieu of the "third man", that product of classical and "Christian" civilization which is embodied in the European spirit with its culture of personality. The structured Church knows how to handle this man, but *only* this man. "Post ecclesiastical man", "fourth man" is beyond its range altogether. In the modern world the current attitude is to count the clergyman (the Church Incarnate) as "an outsider and a stranger", viz., one's association with him is still formalized

[1] See *Theology*, Vol. LXX, No. 568, p. 433 f.

through stereotypes. There is still a place for him as "travelling salesman in solemnities" (Germany), or, if need be, as "the helper of the grave-digger" (France), but he can hardly be a common friend any more. If he wants to become that he will have to be dismantled, and begin to "act normally".'[1] Is it likely that such an outsider will be given a hearing when he preaches? He is not opposed, he is not persecuted; he is tolerated, but he is not taken seriously. What is needed, says Hoekendijk, is not the professional ecclesiastical man, but an apostolate of the laity, small groups entering into no-man's-land, resisting every temptation to engage in an exclusively, or even primarily, verbal communication. Because, through the approach of the word alone, we only reinforce the resistance of the unchurched people, and further foster the bad reputation. Furthermore, apologetics which move on the level of ideology can never serve the communication of the Gospel, because on this level the Gospel will be misunderstood as another 'ideology'.[2] If the pulpit has any future it is as the prompter's box of the laity. 'It is only too bad that the prompter can remain hidden, whereas the man in the pulpit remains so dismally visible, and sometimes annoyingly present.'[3]

Perhaps the question needing to be faced is whether the fate of the ministry of the Word is tied to the structured Church, or could the Word be re-creative of the Church? Is the Word creative?

A *fourth* feature of the modern scene is *the wide gap between technical theology*[4] *and Church proclamation*. The theologians are essential. When a Church's theologians are weak the Church is weak. The theologians conduct the ever-necessary, continuing campaign of casting the Christian 'deposit' or 'tradition' into thought forms meaningful to the modern mind. But preachers

---

[1] *The Church Inside Out*; S.C.M. Press, 1967, p. 51.

[2] Ibid., p. 63.

[3] Ibid., p. 85.

[4] See G. Ebeling, *Theology and Proclamation*; Collins, 1966, p. 14. Also M. Thornton, *The Function of Theology*; Hodder, 1968, p. 14.

14

are also essential. As William Cossor has rightly pointed out, it is not the academic theologians who teach the people.[1] To the parish priests and ministers of the local churches is committed that task. There is, however, a wide gap between the two groups. Here lies a source of the trouble. We have lost the consciousness of theologians and preachers as being members of the one body. It is not that the theologians completely lack a sense of responsibility for the Church's mission, though an outsider could sometimes be pardoned for wondering if this might not be the case. Certainly an absence of pastoral concern could never be laid at the door of Bultmann, Tillich, or J. A. T. Robinson. The disturbing fact of the contemporary situation is, however, that the theologians of the present all too easily, sometimes understandably, fall to scoring off the preachers, thus implying that they are insignificant. The preachers too, for their part, tend to give the impression that they count the work of the theologians as irrelevant to the pulpit. There are many exceptions to this generalization, but the overall picture, whatever the reasons, is that the theologians are not functioning as 'the preachers to the preachers' (Heinrich Ott).[2] Between the two there is a great gap. The theologians work at a high level in an atmosphere which ordinary church congregations with their pastors find too rarefied to breathe. So the pulpit in the modern Church is not renewed by fresh thinking and, what is worse, a feeling is fostered on the part of those few laity who do know something of modern theological insights that preaching is old-fashioned, naïve, little better than nursery moralism.

The question is whether the gap between theologians and preachers is able to be bridged? If not, to see how preaching can survive in the modern world is difficult. And who *should* bridge the gap? Must the congregations in the churches be made theologians? Is this remotely possible? Can the preachers be made theologians? It is estimated that in Germany one-third of the theological students are unable to grasp even what the

[1] *Preaching the Old Testament*; Epworth Press, 1967.
[2] *Theology and Preaching*; Lutterworth Press, 1965, pp. 17–32.

modern theological problems are about. Could it be that the theological colleges stand in the gap between the university theologians and the Church preachers? Are they aware of their task? Or is it that a way must be found by theologians and preachers working together of witnessing to the Christian faith which is so convincingly simple and radical as to overcome problems raised by the tension between the letter and the spirit? And could it be that it is in the realm of Christology that an answer must be found, perhaps through a new understanding of the historical Jesus and his meaning for faith, a relationship on which Bornkamm has much of importance to say – of importance for preaching?

Apart from the form of preaching and the content of preaching there is *one other general feature* of modern life which is inimical to preaching – *the sheer volume of words.* Modern man is tired of them. They stream forth daily from the radios and television sets, they provide cheap reading matter he cannot possibly absorb, they are the stock-in-trade of the recurring conferences on every conceivable subject. Words. Words. Words. Modern man puts his fingers into his ears, or, what is much more likely, he has ceased to listen. When Florrie said to Andy Capp: 'Am I borin' yer?' Andy replied: 'No pet – I'm not listenin'.' The modern spate of words has in itself all but made men deaf. And so the inattentive hearer is prodded with a change of voices to ensure that he will hear; three speakers for a few minutes instead of one speaker for twenty minutes, and the spoken word reinforced by television pictures of the speakers, buttressed up with music and other 'side' effects. 'Battered by words' could be the epitaph over modern man's death to words; words manipulated by propaganda sometimes for evil purposes, words rarely spoken with artistic skill because the snap question and the snap answer is the fashion of the day, words without magic through the sheer prodigality of their modern use. What men today can tune their tired ears and listen to a sermon? It is at best another spate of words.

16

Thus we see preaching at bay, ringed round, maybe, by a fence kept firm by stout poles constituting the objections. Will preaching survive? Will it starve to death in isolation? Or will it escape, passing through the fence because it is a thing no erected barriers can imprison? We must remember preaching has exhibited in the past a surprising power of re-establishing itself; this being the case, the need for examining its essential nature would seem to be pressing. It could be that its nature is such that the objections raised against it cannot wear it down. It escapes to fulfil a role – albeit a changed role – in a new guise, reaching to the end of time. Everything depends, however, on what preaching really is, and where it took its origin.

2.   The Origins of Preaching

THE stakes which fence in preaching, making its continued life questionable, are contemporary objections. They are the oppositions of men whose mid-twentieth-century mood is to question everything, to work in a team, to develop the visual image in communication, to concentrate on speed and to be worn out by the flood of words manipulated for human ends. If preaching is one more activity of merely human origin it would appear to have little hope of survival, ringed round as it is by its rivals.

Suppose, however, for one moment that the origins of preaching lay in the purpose of God, and in some sense it could be described as a divine activity; might it not then be that the human oppositions were ultimately powerless? And if the supposition be counted too absurd to be thinkable, it is no more so than that the Church itself which, seen from the human angle, bears all the marks of human frailty, nevertheless from the divine angle is sufficiently glorious to be called 'the body of Christ'. The Church survives because it is a divine society; in it the divine Spirit lives. Is it possible that likewise preaching is a divine activity? And in it the divine Spirit operates?

In I Corinthians 1:21 we read '. . . it was God's good pleasure through the foolishness of the preaching to save them that believe.' The reference is to 'the thing preached', the *kerugma*, not to the act of preaching (κήρυξις). Is the *act of proclaiming*, however, to be wholly withdrawn from the meaning of *kerugma*?[1] Is not *the action of preaching* part of the saving activity of God? Is it not through the acts of God in history *and* through the continuous proclamation of those acts throughout history *and* through man's appropriation by faith that men are 'saved' (to use Paul's words)? We are not told that it was God's good pleasure through God's saving acts in history to save them that believe, but through those acts proclaimed; in other words, the *kerugma*. Preaching is a *continuation* of God's saving acts in history. In this way it is a divine activity. Bultmann may be wrong to allow only the preached Christ, and not the historical Jesus, as God's saving activity, but he is equally wrong who allows only the historical acts of God, and does not include their proclamation as integral to God's purpose for mankind. Thus preaching is to be counted as more than one among many other human activities; it belongs to the divine purpose. '*It pleased God*,'[2] wrote Paul, 'through the foolishness of the preaching to save them that believe.'

The origins of preaching then do not lie in men, but in God. We cannot therefore begin any inquiry into preaching with a concentration upon the act of preaching represented by the Greek word κήρυξις as if it were in essence oratory, nor upon any human skill, technique or cast of personality. We cannot assert that the first necessity is what the French call *la langue bien pendue*, literally 'the tongue well hung', or the qualities that make for a proficient actor. The latter could be ruinous for preaching. The foundation of preaching is not a human act, nor the proclamation of a human invention, nor even the proclamation of a human discovery. Preaching is in essence the proclamation of something God has done, more particularly

[1] Apparently Samuel Laeuchli in his book *The Language of Faith* (Epworth Press, 1962) does not think so. He writes (p. 246): 'The man who speaks about the foolishness of his language (I Corinthians 1:21) is the man with the most powerful, lively and original speech of the early Church.'

[2] εὐδόκησεν θ -εὸς I Corinthians 1:21; the *N.E.B.* translates 'he chose'.

20

of what God in Christ has done. What gives preaching its significance is not the preacher but what he preaches. This origin the New Testament safeguards by its commonest technical word for preaching, namely, κηρύσσειν, meaning to publish, announce, or proclaim. A clear illustration is seen in Mark 5:20, 'And he began to publish (κηρύσσειν) in Decapolis how great things Jesus had done for him.' This is preaching.

Because of what preaching is, we are plunged into history Preaching is declaring what God *has done* (past tense). We must, however, be careful. 'History itself has no saving power.'[1] Bultmann is right in a sense, the Christ event is history *plus* the preaching of it, *plus* our reception of it through faith. Preaching does not begin in history, it begins in faith. Its roots are in faith. 'We also believe, and therefore also we speak' (II Corinthians 4:13). So it has always been. So it still is. The foundation of preaching is faith; from which it follows that the content of preaching is the Christ of experience and not 'the Jesus of history' (using the term in the nineteenth-century sense). When faith is at a low ebb, preaching is at a low ebb; and conversely, when preaching is at a low ebb, faith is at a low ebb. Preaching and faith are intimately connected. As Canon Douglas Webster has expressed it, 'Preaching and Mission are two thermometers by which to gauge the temperature of a Church.'[2]

Faith, it must be noted, however, is not religious feeling as Schleiermacher taught. It is not this which can be designated the foundation of preaching, or we are back with a human foundation. Faith is essentially decision or response[3] involving the whole personality, the mind, the emotions, and the will. It is decision or response in respect of that which stands over against it. What stood over against the first preachers, that is, the Apostles, was Jesus of Nazareth – his life, his works, his death

[1] Elizabeth Kinniburgh, 'Preaching the Historical Jesus', p. 206. *Theology*, Vol. LXX, No. 563.

[2] College of Preachers' Conference, Swanwick, 1966.

[3] H. F. Lovell Cocks, *By Faith Alone*; James Clarke, 1943, p. 87.

21

and his resurrection. Preaching began in faith as decision, that is, decision *about him*. Preaching has its origin in decision about the Christ event. While, therefore, preaching begins in faith, it is a faith evoked by historical events.

Granted, however, that preaching takes its origin from the faith evoked by the Christ event and is almost a New Testament phenomenon, there are nevertheless *Old Testament antecedents* from which it cannot be separated. Among these the most outstanding is Israel's deliverance from Egypt. This becomes the Old Testament *kerugma*. This was the thing preached. God acted in history at the Red Sea and at Mount Sinai in giving the Law and establishing the Covenant. The Psalmists wax lyrical about this history. The Prophets are the spokesmen of this history. This is the point. For preaching to be understood in the biblical sense there has to be action of God in history, perceived by faith. There have also to be men to interpret God's action. This was the role the prophets came to fulfil. In this way they stand as the precursors of the preachers in the New Testament.

There is even more to it than this. When the eighth-century prophets preached, the creative power of the word was seen. Prophecy did not only interpret history, it *made* history. Words do not only describe what is, they bring into being what hitherto was not. This is another way of saying that words are creative. And so great a hold did this truth take over the minds of the Priestly Writers in Israel that when they produced in the sixth century their account of the divine creation of the world, it appeared in Genesis, Chapter One, as creation *through God's Word*. 'And God said, Let there be . . . and there was . . .' (Genesis 1:3). It was a theme which subsequently became fundamental in the books of the Bible. The Psalmist sings: 'By the Word of the Lord were the heavens made' (33:6). The voice of Deutero-Isaiah cries aloud: 'The grass withereth, the flower fadeth: but the Word of our God shall stand for ever' (40:8). The Synoptists record how Jesus re-created the sick with a word. (Matthew 8:14f.), and the author of I Peter writes: 'Man having

22

been begotten again . . . through the Word of God' (1:23). In the Bible words are never *mere* words. They are effective instruments, an understanding noted by the German word *Ereignis prache*, a 'language event'.

This significance of words grasped through proclamation, notably by the prophets, led to a deeper understanding of the whole significance of language in the life of man. So in Genesis, Chapters Two and Three, it is man who names the animals, it is through speaking that the serpent tempts the woman, and when both man and woman have had a conversation about it and have fallen to temptation, there follows an interchange of words between God and the man. Then in Chapter Eleven of Genesis confusion reigns at the Tower of Babel due to a mis-understanding of language. According to the Bible all the basic experiences of man are connected with words. It is a theme the philosopher Heidegger elaborates.

When we turn to the New Testament we shall find there are *three stages in the development of preaching. Firstly*, John and Jesus suddenly appear as preachers. *Secondly*, there was no preaching of any account till the Christ event was completed. *Thirdly*, preaching did not characterize the Church till after the coming of the Spirit.

At the outset it should be noted that while there is almost a fresh beginning in the history of proclamation when we come to the New Testament, it is not disconnected from its Old Testament antecedents. John the Baptist appears as a 'prophet'. While, however, 'prophecy' continued to play a part in the early Church,[1] it was not this that became characteristic. Prophecy is seen to be losing credit in the pages of the Didache, and it finally ran out in the sands of Montanism in the third century. Preaching, not 'prophecy' (in its narrower and technical sense), is what the Church developed. The word for it, *kerugma*, is almost an exclusively New Testament word. It is used once in the Greek version of the Old Testament for preaching (Jonah 3:2), a

[1] I Corinthians 12:10.

quotation taken up in the New Testament (Matthew 12:41) in one of the seven places where it is used, but that is all. It is true the verb derived from *kerugma* (κηρσσζιν) is used in the Old Testament to translate the Hebrew word for 'call' (קָרָא) but קָרָא has at least seven other meanings besides. In the New Testament, however, the verb 'to proclaim' is used almost exclusively of proclaiming the Gospel. It has become almost a technical word. It is in the light of this that we may say that preaching is a distinctive Christian phenomenon.[1]

This distinctiveness is at once manifest in St Mark's account of the Christ event. Thus he opens his narrative:

> Here begins the Gospel of Jesus Christ the Son of God.
>
> In the prophet Isaiah it stands written: 'Here is my herald whom I send on ahead of you, and he will prepare your way. A voice crying aloud in the wilderness, "Prepare a way for the Lord; clear a straight path for him."' And so it was that John the Baptist appeared in the wilderness proclaiming (κήρνσσων) . . . (Mark 1:1–4; *N.E.B.*).

And as soon as Jesus mounted the stage of public life, and his baptism, anointing by the Spirit, and temptations were over (described by St Mark in five verses) the curtain is lifted on Jesus *as a preacher*:

> After John had been arrested, Jesus came into Galilee proclaiming . . . (Mark 1:14; *N.E.B.*).

This is the point to notice. The new age initiated by John and Jesus began in preaching. John preached. Jesus preached. The close link between these two is important. John was not a mere forerunner announcing the new age to be brought in by Jesus. John *initiated* it.[2] He was the first in the new Christ event, and his work was to proclaim.

[1] 'Preaching. . . is the most distinctive institution in Christianity', P. T. Forsyth, *Positive Preaching and the Modern Mind*; Independent Press, 1953, p. 1.

[2] See Moule, *The Phenomenon of the New Testament*, pp. 70f. Note also in Matthew 11:9–14 how John's work is rooted in Old Testament prophecy. He is 'the destined Elijah' (*N.E.B.*), but he is more than a prophet. Something fresh is present in the new proclamation.

Yet for all the impetus John and Jesus gave to preaching, preaching did not on account of this become characteristic of the early Church. Not even the preaching tours on which Jesus sent the apostles (Luke 9:2) accomplished this. That is to say the apostles did not become preachers *in imitatio Christi*. Not in copying technique, not even the technique of Jesus the preacher, does the foundation of preaching lie. The apostles did not become preachers *until something had happened to the Preacher*. The New Testament *kerugma* did not exist till after another event in history, a bigger event than John and Jesus preaching; the cross and resurrection of Jesus. It is here the origins of preaching lie, in a unique event in history, not simply in a new style of preaching brought in with the coming of Jesus.[1]

We must now turn to look more closely at this unique event. It represents *the second stage* in the history of the development of preaching.

In the nineteenth century there was a diligent search for what was called the 'Jesus of history' – a loaded phrase. It was an activity that failed.[2] The Jesus these 'Questers' found was a simple preacher of the Fatherhood of God and the brotherhood of man. Preaching then was essentially preaching what he preached. Quite apart from questioning whether or not the preaching of Jesus can be summarized in this fashion,[3] the facts are, as has already been stated, that preaching was not engaged in by the apostles *because Jesus preached*, whatever the content; the apostles preached because something happened to Jesus the preacher, namely the cross and the resurrection. In I Corinthians 15:14 St Paul declares what empties preaching of content. It is not the absence of the message Jesus proclaimed, nor is it

---

[1] Mark stresses this new style in the first example he gives of Jesus, synagogue preaching (1:21-28).

[2] How it failed and why it failed has been set out clearly by Professor Dennis Nineham in S.P.C.K. Theological Collections No. 6; *Historicity and Chronology in the New Testament*, Chapter 1 (1965).

[3] It could better be summarized by calling it eschatological – 'the kingdom of God has come'.

the neglect of Jesus' example as a preacher. What gives content
to preaching is his resurrection. 'If Christ hath not been raised,
then is our preaching vain.'[1] Apart from the resurrection preaching lacks its cohesive force.

Moreover, this essential connection between the resurrection
of Jesus and preaching is further demonstrated in the book of the
Acts of the Apostles where Peter is shown to *begin* preaching
because of the resurrection, and to make the resurrection the
burden of his message. Apparently, too, whatever doubts the
Athenians might have nursed concerning Paul's preaching, that
it was about Jesus and resurrection was abundantly clear even
if some did wonder whether *Anastasis*, the word for resurrection,
represented another god or goddess. What this means is that
*preaching without a proclamation of certain historical events is
not possible.* Preaching, on the contrary, even requires a historical tradition to inform it. What this is Paul outlined in
I Corinthians 15:1–8,[2] and the weight is thrown on the resurrection appearances.

At this point Bultmann poses certain important questions,
chief among which (for the purpose of this study) is whether or
not the *historical Jesus* ought to be preached. Bultmann answers
this in the negative. To present the historical Jesus in preaching,
he asserts, is to seek to ground faith in knowledge and thereby
to destroy faith. According to him we must preserve the *Nicht-
sausweisbarkeit*, the unprovability, of Jesus. That there was a
Jesus we cannot doubt. The 'that' of Christ is indeed essential,
but nothing more; nothing about him, nothing about how he
lived, how he preached, how he healed. 'Even though we have
known Christ after the flesh, yet now we know him so no more'
(II Corinthians 5:16). This is not to say that Bultmann does
not preach the cross and the resurrection, but that he does not

---

[1] The word is κενόν and means 'empty'. It is used in Mark 12:3 of the
husbandman who returned to the owner with no produce.

[2] The word 'tradition' is παράδοσις and occurs in Matthew 15:2, 3, 6;
Mark 7:3f.; I Corinthians 11:2; Galatians 1:14; Colossians 2:8; II
Thessalonians 2:15; 3:6.

preach them as historical events. The cross is the picture of the believer's death to himself now, the resurrection is the consequence of that self-dying. Bultmann is concerned for Christian experience, the experience of the living Christ now. It is a truly Christian concern, and no one is going to cast a stone at such a laudable aim who knows to what barrenness the preaching of liberal Protestantism led: it exhausted itself in the search for the Jesus of history along the lines set by Ranke with its overriding canon to discover *Wie es eigentlich gewesen ist* – that is, 'how it actually happened'. In historical research as such is no salvation, even though it be research into the 'original Jesus'.[1]

It could be that Bultmann's denial of a place for the historical Jesus in preaching is counted as a twentieth-century German aberration. Apparently, however, the same tendency appeared in the Corinthian Church. The Corinthian epistles are in fact illuminating on this whole subject of preaching. From I Corinthians 12:1–3 we gather that some people in Corinth were making use of a strange slogan, 'a curse on Jesus!' (*N.E.B.*) Who were these people? Arnold Bittlinger, in his book *Gnadengaben*,[2] after disposing of four possible alternatives, shows that they were Christians; not lapsed Christians, but Christians concerned for the faith. They might almost be called 'super-spiritual' Christians; that is to say, they saw no value for the spiritual life in any concentration on Jesus come in the flesh. What they insisted on was the Christ spirit, the mystical Christ. And they summed up this spiritual concern in one biting phrase, 'a curse on *Jesus*', the emphasis being on Jesus, the historical man. Thus they approached a form of Docetism. Paul met it by his counter phrase, 'No one can say, "*Jesus* is Lord!"' except under the influence of the Holy Spirit.' Here again the emphasis falls on the word *Jesus*. It is the historical man who is called

[1] In the light of this the limitations of such books as Frank Morison's *Who Moved the Stone?* (Faber and Faber, 1930), must be recognized.

[2] Published by Oekumenischer Verlag, Dr R. F. Edel, Marburg an der Lahn, 1966. Translated into English 1967 (Hodder and Stoughton) under the title *Gifts and Graces*. See pp. 17 and 18.

Lord. This confession cannot be deleted from the faith. Echoes of the same conflict are heard in I John 4:2: 'Hereby know ye the Spirit of God: every spirit which confesseth that Jesus Christ is come in the flesh is of God.'

Preaching, therefore, must not be caught in the typically German trap of 'either . . . or': *either* the historical Jesus *or* the Christ of faith. What it must proclaim is *Jesus* as Lord, an insight of faith brought about by the historical resurrection. To preach the Lord Jesus Christ is to preach in the Spirit. This includes the story of the man Jesus of Nazareth. It covers much else, but it is a defect in much modern preaching that this 'old, old story' is not told sufficiently often or convincingly. And if confidence for doing so has been lost on New Testament critical grounds, it could be restored by the work being carried out by Bornkamm and Käsemann, successors to Bultmann, who do not follow his line. And if Professor Moule is correct in suggesting that the synoptic gospels were written to present the historical Jesus as the link between the Church and the world,[1] to neglect him is ruinous for proclamation with evangelistic purpose. Furthermore, in a world where the word 'God' may be meaningless, or at least not meaningful, preaching has an obvious starting-point in the man Jesus.

Preaching is not content to stop with the man Jesus. What it has to proclaim is *the Lord* Jesus. Only because of this faith attitude to him is there preaching at all.[2] The preacher must believe that Jesus is Lord. More than that, he must believe that when he presents Jesus of Nazareth, he is presenting one in whom the Beyond becomes akin. This is the miracle of Jesus of Nazareth. In him the Word of God confronted men in Palestine in 4 B.C. to A.D. 29, or thereabouts. And this is the miracle of preaching, that when Jesus of Nazareth is proclaimed from faith in him as Lord, the Word of God still

[1] *The Phenomenon of the New Testament*, Appendix II; S.C.M. Press, 1967.

[2] This is why conservative evangelical preaching, which tends to multiply the titles of Jesus, is more right than wrong, and achieves results.

confronts men. This is not a proposition that can be proved. That Jesus is both 'very man' and 'very God' remains for ever the stumbling block of the Catholic faith. Neither is there any way of logic from *vere homo* to *vere Deus*, only the way of faith. But the preacher must believe in the possibility of the miracle. He must believe that in proclaiming Jesus as Lord, God encounters men.[1] This is the *sine qua non* of preaching. This is what is meant by proclaiming Christ. This is the foundation of preaching.

Preaching, then, has its origin not simply in Jesus as a preacher, but in the faith evoked by what happened to Jesus the preacher, chiefly his resurrection; preaching has its origin in the faith that he is Lord.

St Paul said that no one can say 'Jesus is Lord!' except under the influence of the Holy Spirit. It is also historically true that Jesus was not actually proclaimed as Lord except under the influence of the Holy Spirit. This is striking. What it means is that although the founder of Christianity was a preacher; although, too, something startling happened to this preacher, namely his resurrection after crucifixion; that is to say, although there was something to announce, although there was a *kerugma*, acts of preaching did not take place on any significant scale *till the coming of the Spirit*. If, then, Jesus as a preacher is the first fact which lies at the origin of preaching, and if what happened to this preacher at Calvary is the second fact which lies at the origin of preaching, the third fact is the coming of the Spirit. To this we turn.

Apostolic preaching began on the day of Pentecost. According to Acts 1:5 the promise had been given: 'You will be baptized with the Holy Spirit, and within the next few days' (*N.E.B.*). Up to that time the Spirit was 'not yet', to use a phrase from the Fourth Gospel. But when the Spirit came, all at once preaching

---

[1] 'Encounter with the man Jesus means encounter with him who came to expression in him.' G. Ebeling, *Theology and Proclamation*; Collins, 1966, p. 79.

was everywhere. It is scattered over the pages of the New Testament. Peter was up on his feet on the day of Pentecost. Stephen, set apart 'to serve tables', nevertheless preached. Laymen scattered abroad preached in the lands of their dispersion. Paul encompassed a great part of the Roman Empire, preaching. And St Luke, in the book of the Acts of the Apostles, gives examples of what they preached. And if it cannot be claimed that what the records present is the actual words of apostolic sermons, it is certainly the preaching of the very early Church. Apparently such preaching began in Jerusalem and reached to Rome, the universal city. So preaching is presented as a universal activity of the Church. It was what the Spirit-guided Church felt to be the will of Jesus. As the shorter ending of St Mark's Gospel expresses it: 'Afterwards Jesus himself sent out ($\dot{\epsilon}\xi\alpha\pi\dot{\epsilon}\sigma\tau\epsilon\iota\lambda\epsilon\nu$) by them from east to west the sacred and imperishable message (*kerugma*) of eternal salvation.' It was to be an activity till the end of time. 'And this Gospel of the Kingdom will be proclaimed throughout the earth as a testimony to all nations; and then the end will come' (Matthew 24:14; *N.E.B.*, see also Mark 13:10). Preaching thus belongs to the dispensation of the Spirit. The era of the Spirit is the era of preaching. The manifestation of the Spirit of God is the foundation of preaching. It is in Pentecost that the origins of preaching must be sought.

What is the action of the Spirit in preaching?

The words of Jesus as reported in the Fourth Gospel give the first answer to this question: '. . . When he comes who is the Spirit of truth. . . . He will glorify me, for everything that he makes known to you he will draw from what is mine' (John 16:13–14; *N.E.B.*). On this Temple comments: 'For what the Spirit does is not to impart knowledge of other themes or future events but to interpret Christ.'[1] The Spirit, then, is pre-eminently *the Interpreter*. He is the divine Hermeneut. He opens up the Scripture,[2] he opens up contemporary events in the light of the

---

[1] William Temple, *Readings in St John's Gospel*; Macmillan, 1942, p. 292.

[2] The Greek word is $\delta\iota\alpha\nuο\dot{\iota}\gamma\omega$ (Luke 24:31, 32, 45).

Scriptures, he opens up the significance of the Christ, he opens up the mind, just as the Risen One did on the Emmaus Road. The Spirit makes the hearers of preaching perceive, as did the Risen Christ on the Emmaus Road, the necessity of the cross. 'Was the Messiah not bound to suffer thus . . .?' (Luke 24:26; *N.E.B.*). Preaching has its origin then where the Spirit interprets Christ. It does not begin simply where knowledge of the historical Jesus exists. It begins with baptism in the Spirit, that Spirit who is the interpreter of the historic Jesus. There was not, there is not, preaching without the Holy Spirit.

The Spirit also *quickens* men. The Spirit does something to men's tongues. The account of the Day of Pentecost in the book of the Acts of the Apostles is largely about speaking. It was the speaking and the manner of it on the part of the Apostles that drew the crowds. It made them know that a new spiritual power was at work. The manner of the preaching suggested a Real Presence. Apparently the life of a Church is known by its preaching. It is an indication of a Church's temperature. And when preaching is 'in the Spirit' it conveys meaning. 'How is it then that we hear them, each of us in his own native language?' the crowds asked as a result of the Apostolic preaching on the Day of Pentecost. Peter explained that it was the result of the coming of the Spirit. The Spirit is the interpreter. Meaningful preaching results from his presence. This is why elocution does not lie at the foundation of preaching, but *the Spirit interpreting the Christ event through the quickened lips of men baptized in the Spirit*. Then new patterns of speaking evolve, needing discipline, no doubt, as St Paul insists in connection with 'the tongues movement'; but without the activity of the Spirit training and techniques will accomplish little, and may even be offensive.

Preaching today is ringed round with hostilities and difficulties, the product of the times; so ringed round that it would appear as if its day is done. But this can only be if preaching is in essence human oratory. So to understand it, however, is to *mis*understand. *Preaching has its roots in a divine purpose for*

31

mankind made visible in Jesus as Lord interpreted by the divine Spirit. To the eye of faith, therefore, it is a divine activity, and as such can be expected to break human barriers to perform its saving work till the end of time, though doubtless changing its forms and patterns as need arises.

3. The Content of Preaching

IN the previous chapter the point was made that the origins of preaching do not lie in human oratory; they do not lie in the human at all, they lie in the actions of God in history perceived by faith. It is in the uniqueness of those events, and in particular in the uniqueness of the Christ event that the justification for the practice of preaching exists. To express the matter bluntly, because of what God has done, men preach.

But what has God done? How are we informed of the divine action in history? How is there content in preaching unless something to meet that need is *given*?

The short answer to these questions is – the Bible; and the elaboration of that answer is the substance of this chapter. It is the Bible that gives content to preaching. And not only content, but form also. That is to say, not only is there provided in the Bible something to communicate, but also a language *by which it is communicated*. That such a provision is made is not surprising. Anything unique must have a unique conveyor if it is to be conveyed, and God's actions in history, especially the Christ event, are certainly unique.

First then, in our consideration of the Bible, we turn our attention to *language*. At first this seems strange, if not illogical. The proper course would seem to be to consider first *what* is to be preached, and when that is settled, *how* it is to be preached.

In other words, content must precede form. But this is not so. Form affects content. It so affects it that there has been provided not only a Gospel but also a language by which to communicate it. Both content and form belong to the given things which the preacher must use.

What this given language is has been explained by Dr Alan Richardson. He writes:

It is important that we should understand what is meant by speaking the language which the Bible has created. The emphasis does not lie here on the formal side, as when we say that a poet creates his own language. The biblical writers are not aiming at imparting a new doctrine or describing a religious experience. The process is more like the way in which a scientist makes his own scientific language: in order to describe with sufficient exactness, science must invent an ever-lengthening list of new technical expressions and symbols. Ordinary speech is not adequate or precise enough to serve the purpose of scientific description of natural processes. However remote the symbols of science may seem to the layman (such as the square root of minus one), they are grounded in something outside the imagination of the scientist, they correspond to something in the nature of things, and thus we may say that the subject-matter of science creates a scientific language. In a similar way the biblical theology must create its own terminology which is bound to appear technical to the layman; but it should be noted that, as in the case of science, the technical nature of the term is the result of the structure of events outside the imagination of the theologian and corresponds to something in the nature of the real. Ordinary everyday speech is not precise enough to serve the purpose of theological understanding.

The Bible was not written by men who had sat down to think out a new doctrine or idea of God. It was written by men who had observed or participated in epoch-making events and who had perceived the significance of those events. The words which the biblical writers came to use received their own special impress on the mould of real events. The biblical words are, as it were, a coinage stamped at the mint of history. They are not simply expressing ideas in the mind of a poet or philosopher: their purpose is to hand on a message about something which has taken place. God has brought up his people out of Egypt. He has restored the exiles who had languished in Babylon. He has visited and redeemed his people in Jesus Christ. The words refer to actual things which have been done, to facts of sacred history. The New Testament points on every page to what God has done in Christ. This central fact creates a new language and no other language is adequate to express it.[1]

What this means is that not only every preacher, but every Christian, has to learn a new language. He cannot be a Christian without at least a smattering of this new tongue. What is implied, of course, is not Hebrew or Greek, but the divine language which lies behind what is expressed when God's actions are described, be it in Hebrew, Greek, Finnish or Urdu. There are words like 'righteousness', 'sin', 'judgement', 'salvation', and 'repentance' which simply do not carry the same meaning in the language of faith as, for instance, in a news column. A Christian has to learn the Christian meanings.

If then Christian language lessons, however elementary, are necessary for ordinary Christian men, Christian language study is essential for those whose calling it is to preach. On these grounds it could be said with justification that the greatest contribution of a basic nature to the preacher's needs has been the massive theological dictionary produced in Germany by Kittel, his successors and colleagues.[2] The point here is of immense importance. At a time when the Church is conscious of its failure to communicate its message, it may so concentrate on becoming involved with those to whom it has to communicate that it fails to achieve a thorough acquaintance with *what* it has to communicate; and this means not only the record of God's actions in history but the language which essentially belongs to that record and is part of what is given.

Secondly, we turn to *the communication* of the divine language;

[1] Alan Richardson, *Preface to Bible Study*; S.C.M. Press, 1943, pp. 85–87.
[2] The *Theologisches Wörterbuch zum neuen Testament*, Stuttgart, 1933.

35

for the recognition of it and the learning of it do not complete the preacher's task. He still must learn to communicate, for if it is not communicated it will be a dead language. Immediately he begins to undertake the task, however, he is involved in the clash of language. For example, the word 'love' bears one meaning in the biblical language and a very different meaning in the framework of the film industry. So preaching involves the struggle of interpretation from one language to another. And the struggle never ceases. Each epoch speaks a language of its own. And in any one epoch different groups use different frameworks of speech. Moreover, the preacher himself, belonging to a particular epoch, has his own 'mother framework' of speech.

One of the most common contemporary frameworks of speech is that which derives from the dominance of science and technology. What modern men utter is the language of scientifically-conditioned thinking. Another framework is the language of economics. The twentieth-century problem of the preacher, therefore, is how to translate the language of faith into these frameworks. And the labour is not only finding the right equivalents so that *meaningful* words about the Gospel are spoken, but also words that will not *distort* what is meant by the words in the divine language.

This is not a new problem. It arose very early in the history of the Christian Church. By the second century the Church was 'up to its eyes' in this struggle. It arose over Gnosticism, and it is in this struggle that we see for the first time most clearly what is meant by the clash of language. The Gnostics sought to convey the Christian message to the men of their time, and to do so they used not only the divine language, but the language frameworks of that time. In doing so, however, they altered the meanings of the words in the divine language, till in the end they were preaching 'another Gospel'. An example is the use of the word 'father'. It occurs four hundred times in the New Testament. It is a New Testament word with a distinctive New Testament meaning which has to be learnt. The Gnostics, however, so used it in deference to the thought forms of their contemporaries that it ceased to carry the meaning of a *personal* father. Through loss of concreteness it became an abstraction, and 'the father' was finally presented as the highest stage in the universe. This is not what the New Testament says.

Professor Laeuchli has traced five steps in the transformation from Christian to Gnostic speech through which the distinctive Christian message is lost.[1]

1. Language about Jesus Christ is no longer concrete. He has no flesh and blood. He does not dwell among men.
2. Man becomes the battle-ground between flesh and spirit, he is not a unity. This is because the biblical Hebraic understanding of man is abandoned.
3. Biblical realism is replaced by symbolism.
4. The Old Testament is rejected and with it the notion of God as creator and one who has dealings with man.
5. There is no community of faith on earth, the ecclesia is an aeon, pre-existent and heavenly.

All this represents a list of losses brought about by a failure in the second century to interpret the divine language into the speech of the contemporary world *without distorting it*.

The twentieth-century Church is also 'up to its eyes' in the same problem. It is witnessing various attempts to translate the Christian Gospel into words that are meaningful to twentieth-century man. The need arises in particular because modern man has been trained in observing phenomena, and so has built up a corpus of knowledge constantly verified by experiment. Knowledge for him is almost equivalent to 'know-how'. God, however, is not a 'thing' about which there can be 'know-how'. He may be related to 'things', but according to theism he is Other than *all* things. If, therefore, knowledge really is the 'know-how' which twentieth-century man, scientifically conditioned, takes it to be, God simply does not fit into the pattern of knowledge at all. He is not 'knowable'. He is not there. As David Jenkins has expressed the point, 'the debate about God

[1] *The Language of Faith*; Epworth, 1962, pp. 73–88.

is really a confrontation between the undoubted givenness of that with which the scientist deals and – what?'[1]

How is the interpretation of the language of faith made to these people? Attempts are made. We have translators. They are not to be underrated. They are doing essential Christian work. They are committed to the Christian mission; but the question must always be asked of each one: In translating the message into contemporary speech, is he distorting it? Part of the terror of the situation is that quite often an answer can only be given after the passage of time during which much damage may be done. No doubt Friedrich Schleiermacher, preaching to the 'cultured despisers of religion' in Berlin at the dawn of the nineteenth century, seemed really to communicate the Gospel in that scientific and cultured milieu. We now see, however, that in asserting that the root of religion is in 'feeling' about God, and not in reason or revelation, Schleiermacher put God at the mercy of man. Similarly, Barth seemed to be voicing the speech proper to twentieth-century man in the years following the First World War, but are we sure that he has not distorted the message of the Bible? Bultmann longed above all else to address the men of the post-Second World War period, but is it the New Testament Gospel he preaches? The same question may be asked of Tillich and Bonhoeffer. And are we *quite* sure that for all the hearing that Bishop Robinson has received, he has not reduced the Christian Gospel to Humanism with Christian overtones? Or to pinpoint the question: In proclaiming God as 'the ground of man's being', is this really the same God as the One who, according to the Bible, especially the Old Testament, has relations of a personal nature with man? We must respect these men. They have entered into the conflict of language from which many have held back, but it is by no means certain that they have won the battle *for the language of faith*. In any case it is a battle that has constantly to be re-fought.

Thirdly, we are brought to consider *the Canon of Holy Scripture*. We are brought to this point through the necessity of asking

[1] *Guide to the Debate about God*; Lutterworth, 1966, p. 19.

if there is 'a measuring tape' for the language of faith. How do we know whether or not speech by any particular man or group of men, even when preaching what seems to be Christianity, is in fact truly Christian speech? To answer this question we return to the second century.

It has already been pointed out that the Gnostics distorted the meanings of 'Christian' words like 'father' when they communicated them, because of the language they used. It is, however, important to observe as well that *they did use* the language of faith even if in translating it they distorted it. In fact they quoted it extensively. But what is its origin? How do we know what *is* the language of faith? Is there 'a measuring tape' by means of which it can be assessed?

At the time of the Gnostics the words of Jesus and of the Apostles, especially Paul and John, were in circulation as a living tradition. There were also the Hebrew Scriptures in writing, but the Gnostics quickly rejected the latter as not being susceptible to their handling. Marcion's attitude to the Old Testament is well-known. The language of faith, however, that was in circulation in the form of dominical and apostolic words, was taken as the basis of the Gnostic preaching. It is important to observe that the Gnostics were clear about the need for a divine language. There has to be something to translate. The question, however, is: what is the 'something'? What is its origin? What are the limits? By whom is it accepted? It was over against the Gnostics that the Canon of Holy Scripture began to be formulated, finally comprising the books of the New Testament as we have now received them, and including what are now called the Old Testament Scriptures. This is the Canon, this is the rule, this is 'the measuring tape' by which speech purporting to be Christian speech is judged.

What this means is that the language of faith has to be biblical; the divine language is biblical language; and Christian preaching, to be Christian, has to be biblical, that is, true to the Bible. It is because Gnosticism failed *at this point* that it failed altogether.

But what do we mean by 'true to the Bible'? We mean true

to the framework in which the divine language operates, true to the central theme of the Bible, and to the comprehension of the whole. We do not mean true to this or that text illuminated by the Spirit. Such was the Gnostic approach to the Bible which ended in distortion. It was a fundamentalist approach. True to the Bible means true to the Bible's way of speaking about the Incarnate God, it means christological language within the Hebraic concept of the relation between God and man. It is *kerugmatic* language, a language of movement oscillating between grace and demand, between the past and the future. It is vibrant, highly artistic, and realistic. Being true to the Bible means being true to this canonical language.

To become untrue to the Bible – that is, for Christian speech to lose informing contact with canonical language – is all too easy. It is what happened in the sub-apostolic history of the Church. Then transmission of boring theology takes the place of dynamic proclamation, and orthodox language may even become a whip by which ecclesiastical authority can be asserted. So weariness and deadness is the experience of the Church, brought about by the loss of touch with the unique speech of the canon. Fortunately the loss has never been complete. Laeuchli has shown how it was preserved in the second century in the work of Ireneus. Granted Ireneus's speech was poor, granted it was too often too polemical, it nevertheless did reflect the tension of the Gospel, and it did operate between the Greek language of ontology and the Hebraic speech of the Old Testament without giving way to either. It was informed by canonical language though reaching out to contemporary hearers. Laeuchli also quotes from the example of the preaching of Melito, the second century Bishop of Sardis in Lydia.[1] Here we see a form of address which is personal, lyrical and lively. It has a richness of imagery and a vivid reference to the newness of life Christ has brought. This is second-century speech communicating divine or canonical speech. This is Christian preaching.

Fourthly, we are now in a position to answer the question,

[1] *The Language of Faith*, p. 228.

'what is the content of preaching?' by giving the short answer, *the message of the Bible*. This word 'message' is deliberately chosen as the most comprehensive term available for the whole range of that which it is the business of the Christian ministry to convey to the faithful, and to the world in general so far as it will hear. In the New Testament various terms are employed bringing into view one aspect or another of 'the message':

1. *Kerugma* (κήρυγμα) that is, the public proclamation of the Gospel.
2. *Martyria* (μαρτυρία) that is, testimony to facts for which the witness accepts responsibility.
3. *Didache* (διδαχή) that is, teaching, including:
   (*a*) the development of truths contained in the *kerugma*;
   (*b*) ethical instruction deduced from the *kerugma*;
   (*c*) *parangeliai* (παραγγελία) that is, specific maxims (*praecepta*) resulting from that instruction.

All these are included in the word 'message'.[1]

Among the various terms *kerugma* is basic because it is regulative of the whole New Testament,[2] giving it a unity of theme. What it consists of was worked out by C. H. Dodd in what he called *The Apostolic Preaching and its Development*.[3] That the main points have recently been incorporated in a lecture by Professor Dodd himself in a Roman Catholic publication on preaching bearing the Imprimatur of the Vicar-General of Westminster,[4] is evidence of how non-sectarian but truly catholic are Dr Dodd's insights into the nature of the *kerugma*, even if some of his points need qualifying.

What is the core of the *kerugma*? It is a brief recital of the Christian historical facts, but it is not a bare account. It is so set out that the significance of those events is indicated.

[1] Cf. Essay by C. H. Dodd in *The Ministry of the Word*; ed. Paulinus Milner; Burns and Oates, 1967, p. 45.
[2] See R. H. Fuller, *The New Testament in Current Study*; S.C.M. Press, 1963, pp. 9 and 10.
[3] Published by Hodder and Stoughton, 1936.
[4] *The Ministry of the Word* (see above).

1. There is the theme of fulfilment. Christ's coming is the consummation of God's dealings with Israel in the past to which the prophets bore witness. (Thus the Old Testament is bound into the preaching.)

2. Because Christ has come, men now stand within the new age of salvation which the prophets hoped for, but which is now an actuality. (Thus the facts about Jesus are not mere facts, they tell of how that which is beyond history has entered history.)

3. Since the age of salvation is present, men are invited to accept the offer of forgiveness of sins and to enter into the community of those who are empowered by the Holy Spirit, the Spirit of Christ.

The content of preaching is, therefore, the content of the Bible. Preaching is exposition but – and this is of paramount importance – *it is exposition in the light of the kerugma*. It is this kind of exposition that is true to the Bible, for the New Testament as a whole is an expansion and application of the *kerugma*, and the Old Testament is brought into oneness with the New because the latter fulfils it. *The content of preaching, therefore, is the whole Bible expounded in the light of the kerugma.*[1] Preaching and the Bible are tied together. And the Church tradition in which sermons begin with a text is a witness to this connection, though all too often the connection is hard to perceive in the oration which follows.

Fifthly, we might turn now to consider one particular fact among the historical facts which are recited and form the core of the *kerugma*, namely, *the resurrection of Jesus*. We must do this because it has a special relationship to preaching. In I Corinthians 15:14 we have Paul's categorical statement, 'If Christ hath not been raised, then is our preaching vain'; that is, 'empty'. The resurrection of Jesus, therefore, gives content to

[1] The unifying *theology* (that is, the *kerugma*) underlying the diverse literary elements in the Old Testament is where John Bright finds the authority of the Old Testament for the Church and for preachers. See his important book *The Authority of the Old Testament*; S.C.M. Press, 1967.

preaching. It is a point we have already made.[1] It still stands, but difficulties arise. How are we to *interpret* the resurrection of Jesus? Is not this the terror of the situation? If we are unsure of the resurrection what have we to proclaim? Have we not come to the end of the road as far as preaching is concerned?

Here care must be taken to differentiate between the fact of the resurrection and how it actually happened.[2] We do not know *how it actually happened.* The Gospel records do not attempt to describe this aspect. What they give is the testimony of various witnesses whose experiences on Easter Day and subsequently, at the grave where Jesus was buried and elsewhere, led them to the conviction that he had risen from the dead. *Christians must believe in the resurrection of Christ.* How it happened is a matter concerning which there must be allowed a difference of opinion. If Professor Lampe is able to think that the bones of Jesus lie buried somewhere in Palestine and yet to believe firmly, as he does, in the resurrection of Christ, basing his conviction on the appearances of Jesus, this view must be respected. Those who without specifying such a spiritual resurrection assert that something did happen, but what it was does not matter – the important thing is to believe that Christ is not dead but risen – must likewise be respected. Whether, however, the view that obtained in some Church circles between the wars, that what the resurrection expresses is the resurrection of the Apostles' *faith*, whether this view can be respected as a legitimate variant, is doubtful. What is essential is a belief in the resurrection *of Christ*.

We must recognize that there are difficulties in all descriptions of the resurrection, including the orthodox. There are *literary* difficulties in the New Testament stories which may or may not be capable of harmonization. In all this, in the last resort, there may not be a wiser course than to accept the biblical accounts as the best possible attempts at describing what is ultimately

[1] *Supra*, p. 25.
[2] The phrase in German, *wie es eigentlich gewesen ist*, is almost a technical expression since Ranke, the nineteenth-century German historian, made this a key of historical method.

indescribable. That is to say, we accept them not because their evidence is incontrovertible. From the Bible we are not encouraged to think that God ever provides incontrovertible evidence of his presence or actions. We are not given data that will lead to knowledge. We are, however, given sufficient evidence to make the leap of faith into the dark reasonable; that is, the leap of faith into belief in Christ's resurrection from the dead. In this way we can receive the facts of the Gospel which have been handed down to us, as St Paul did (I Corinthians 15:3–7). And thus believing in the resurrection, there is something to preach; preaching is not empty, it has content.

This means that our message is not 'the Jesus of history' so avidly sought by the nineteenth-century Liberal Protestants under the impression that if only they could unwrap the ecclesiastical Christ and the Christ of dogma from all that hid the 'real' Jesus, they would be in touch with the secret of his person. It was a quest which failed.[1] Nor, on the other hand, is our message simply 'the Christ of experience', the unsatisfactoriness of which is being shown by the successors to Bultmann in Germany in their re-emphasis on Jesus of Nazareth. *The content of our preaching is the man Jesus declared to be the Lord Jesus by the resurrection from the dead.*

It is in meeting this Jesus, it is through confrontation by this Jesus that 'God comes to expression'.[2] Nowhere does this confrontation take place so meaningfully as at the cross of Christ. It is there that men are brought to the end of themselves, it is there that we are brought to the limit of our ability to count this man as one of ourselves. He is with us in our predicament, but he stands over against us in the way he faces it. If up to this point we think we have fathomed Jesus, we can fathom him no

[1] How and why it failed has been set out by Professor D. Nineham in S.P.C.K. *Theological Collections*, No. 6, 1965, 'Historicity and Chronology of the New Testament'.

[2] The phrase is that of Gerhard Ebeling. See *Theology and Proclamation*, p. 79. He writes, 'Implicit Christological *kerugma* is the word-event in which the encounter with Jesus brings God to expression in the reality in which we live.'

more at the cross. It is here that we sense we are confronted by Another, by the Other come to meet us from the Beyond. Because this happens pre-eminently at the cross, it was the burden of Paul's preaching. 'We preach Christ crucified,' he wrote, 'Christ the power of God, and the wisdom of God' (I Corinthians 1:23, 24). And so confident was he that the mystery of God was revealed at this place, that in his ministry to the Corinthians, an eminently fruitful ministry, he determined to know nothing else 'save Jesus Christ, and him crucified' (I Corinthians 2:2, 3).

This then is the faith of the preacher in the content of his message, that in proclaiming Christ, the crucified and risen Lord, God will 'come to expression' to men now. The preacher cannot *make* that confrontation take place, he can only preach in the faith that it will take place if he proclaims. It is a faith peculiar to the preacher, but without it he is no proper preacher. It is preaching under the conviction of the existence of the transcendent. Herein lies the mystery and miracle of preaching. It is not wholly explicable in human terms, which is why the oppositions that ring it round cannot be final.

4. The Form of Preaching

In the previous chapter the question was asked, 'What is the content of preaching?' From the short answer that was given, namely, the message of the Bible, it might be inferred that preaching is essentially the explanation of that message in as clear and intelligent terms as possible. The preacher who can 'get across' to his own generation biblical doctrine is fulfilling his role.

But this view is based on a misunderstanding. The revelation of God contained in the Bible has not been given in the form of a set of doctrinal propositions waiting for the preacher's elucidation and translation into modern thought and language patterns. Preaching cannot, therefore, be conceived of in these terms. And when it is, even by those who are anything but fundamentalists, there is betrayed a confusion of thought about the mode of revelation. This confusion is evident in much of the loose talk about 'the teaching sermon', and about the problem of communication. As R. E. C. Browne has expressed it, 'There can be no great preaching whenever the question, "Is there a knowledge of reality which can neither be perceived nor expressed in propositional form?" is unasked or left unanswered.'[1]

The primary concern of the preacher is not to impart doctrine, certainly not to make people believe it as he believes it; the

[1] *The Ministry of the Word*; S.C.M. Press, 1958, p. 7.

47

primary concern of the preacher is to interpret life so that his hearers may find their own satisfying answers in God. And if this is a true description of what the aim of preaching should be, some of the modern criticism directed against it, already described,[1] either rests on a misunderstanding of what preaching is, or has been formulated as a result of preaching which is not proper preaching. It is criticism misplaced. Preaching is not indoctrination by an authority, it is interpretation of life. This is why to resist preaching may involve restriction to narrowness of vision.

This does not imply that doctrine is no concern of the preacher. On the contrary, every preacher must be a theologian. The preacher, however, must understand what doctrine is. It is a means of bearing with the complexity of life; its freedom and its determinism, its life and its death, its pleasure and its pain, its joy and its sorrow – without 'going under'. Doctrine is not a set of fixed answers no experience can disturb; it is a way of interpreting experience, sufficient to provide enough light by which to live. The preacher *struggles* with doctrine, sometimes *against* doctrine. This is because he works close to life, and senses the prior claims of life over doctrine but, because he works so close to life, or to that part of it he experiences, he does not often see it whole. This partial view of life is one reason why the effective preacher often sits awkwardly with orthodoxy. To love people is to strain at doctrine, but doctrine cannot be jettisoned like useless cargo. It must be understood for what it is, a rough sketch map of the awkward terrain of human existence.

Perhaps we are now in a position to affirm what preaching is *not*.

It is *not essentially a means of providing information*, not even information about God or, to express the matter more strongly, *certainly* not information about God, for God is not 'a thing'. As Dr Coggan has expressed it: 'Jesus, so the Gospels would seem to indicate, was not at pains to lecture to his disciples

[1] Supra, p. 5.

about God.'[1] The only way in which preaching is informing
about God is the way the 'Schoolmen' used the word; it is
speaking so that God is *formed in* the hearers, that is, God gives
inner form to them. But preaching is not lecturing. It is not
providing information. That is to say, the provision of information is not the aim of preaching. This is true even though information may actually be conveyed. Nor must we run to the
opposite extreme and assess preaching in emotional terms.
Preaching is neither an intellectual exercise nor an emotional
exercise; it partakes of both; and if it does not it will fail. If
preaching has *no more* than an emotional appeal, it will leave
nothing behind it but a thirst for more sensation. If it has *no
more* than an intellectual appeal, it will not receive prolonged
attention, for people must *feel* interested in what they hear. In
point of fact, there are no purely intellectual hearers or purely
emotional hearers. We must be careful, therefore, how we talk
about 'a teaching sermon', and we must certainly not equate
preaching with lecturing.

Nor is preaching propaganda. This is brought out in the first
chapter of St Mark's Gospel. In that chapter we are introduced
to preaching as one of the characteristics of the Messianic age
that dawned with John the Baptist. We are given the content of
the preaching, the authority of the preaching, the power of the
preaching, and the effect of the preaching. What was also offered
was propaganda, but not by Jesus. There was an unclean spirit
that cried out, 'I know who you are – the Holy One of God'
(Mark 1:24; *N.E.B.*). But Jesus rebuked it, silenced it and
exorcized it. And throughout his ministry Jesus continued as
'the secret Messiah'. Far from engaging in personal propaganda,
far from advertising and pressing upon the public any claims to
divinity, he went so far as to hide it under enigmatic titles such
as 'the Son of Man', and to encourage silence upon the part of
those who would make him known (Mark 1:43). The triumphal
entry of Jesus into Jerusalem is largely significant because it
stands out in contrast from the uniform synoptic portrait of

[1] *The Prayers of the New Testament*; Hodder and Stoughton, 1967, p. 87.

Jesus, of one whose life was consciously hidden under 'the form of a servant'. He preached; but there was no propaganda for himself, for the Twelve, for the larger body of his disciples, for Israel, or even for God. What Jesus sought was to share his own experience of God with others. Preaching belonged to this aim. It was not propaganda.

Preaching is not moralizing. Because a great many people think it is, and because preaching has too often been presented as if it were moralizing, there has developed a great weariness with preaching. Jesus, however, was a preacher, but he was no moralizer. Otherwise he would have had more to say to the paralytic than: 'My son, your sins are forgiven' (Mark 2:5; *N.E.B.*). Jesus did not gloss over sin, he was ready to expose sin as in his sermon in the Nazareth synagogue (Luke 4:24–27) and in his challenge to the 'doctors of the law' and the Pharisees at Jerusalem (Matthew 23:1–23); but his aim was not moral reformation, it was to tear down the shutters behind which men live with the result that they do not see God as Jesus saw him, nor let themselves be seen by God as they really are. Jesus came for judgement, but it was not the judgement of moralizing, nor was it in order to achieve conformity to ethical conventions. The mission of Jesus was a judgement that '(gives) sight to the sightless and (makes) blind those who see' (John 9:39; *N.E.B.*). Jesus' first concern was with seeing, it was not with behaviour.

If, then, preaching does not take the form of lecturing, propaganda or moralizing, what form does it take? What is preaching proper?

Preaching is proclamation *through a person*.[1] Once more it is St Mark who gives a basic example. Of the cured madman of Gerasa we read, 'The man went off and spread the news (ἤρξατο κηρύσσειν) in the Ten Towns of all that Jesus had done for him...' (Mark 5:20; *N.E.B.*). This is the most elementary form of proclamation through a person. It is, in fact, personal testimony. The healed man tells of what things Jesus has done for *him*. So

[1] This is a sharper version of Phillips Brooks's phrase 'truth through personality'.

also the man born blind, who washed in the pool of Siloam at Jesus' bidding, testified, 'He spread a paste on my eyes; then I washed, and now I can see' (John 9:15; *N.E.B.*). There is no doubt that personal testimony must be an initial experience for the preacher. It may not be experience of a bodily healing, nor of a religious conversion; it may be a vision such as Isaiah recounted: 'In the year that King Uzziah died I saw the Lord sitting upon a throne...' (Isaiah 6:1); or a voice calling, 'Whom shall I send, and who will go for us?'; or even the consciousness of divine words implanted in the inner being: 'Son of man, eat that thou findest; eat this roll, and go, speak unto the house of Israel' (Ezekiel 3:1). Whatever its nature, it is experience in some form *of God*. This must be the initial experience to which the preacher can testify.

Personal testimony, however, is not the whole of that which is meant by preaching being described as proclamation *through a person*. What is meant is personal involvement. The preacher is involved in the message he is proclaiming. The message is involved in his personality as he proclaims it. The preacher does not stand back from his message. He does not reach for it and hand it over to his hearers as if he were a shopkeeper; it passes through him. It becomes *part* of him before he *imparts* it. The Word becomes flesh, his flesh, the flesh of the preacher. John B. Smith with his ginger hair, stubby fingers and fine bass voice. When he preaches, it is the gospel according to John B. Smith. It will not have the same emphasis or colours as the gospel according to Harry A. Dennis, but it will be the gospel shining through each of these preachers, distorted, maybe, incomplete, no doubt, but it will be *the gospel proclaimed through a person*.[1] Only once did the Word of God shine in pure clarity through a person; this was Jesus, the Word of God become flesh, who

---

[1] The two examples given are male. Fullness of proclamation cannot however take place unless there is also proclamation through female personality. It is this which gives the books *The Transformation of Man* (Chapman, 1967), and *Why be a Christian?* (Chapman, 1968) by Rosemary Haughton, their distinctive quality.

dwelt among men, and in whom was seen the glory of 'the only begotten of the Father, full of grace and truth' (John 1:14). But whenever a man preaches, the Word of God is enfleshed, there is proclamation through a person, weak, sinful, fallible and gifted. Preaching is a highly personal form of proclamation, different from lecturing, conducting propaganda or moralizing; the preacher is part of his message, so much so that he is even preaching when he is not in his pulpit.

There is a story of St Francis of Assisi who summoned a young man to accompany him on a preaching mission to a village. They passed along one street, then another and another, St Francis the while talking and engaging the young man in conversation. After a time the young man inquired, 'But when are we to begin the preaching?' To which St Francis replied, 'All the time we have been walking up and down in conversation with each other, people have been watching us. Thus we have preached our sermon.'

From the fact that preaching is essentially proclamation through a person, certain conclusions follow. One conclusion is that *there are no two preachers exactly alike.* This is because there are no two persons exactly alike. Human beings are different from each other down to the tips of their fingers, as every criminal and criminologist knows. There are no 'repeats' or copies among persons. Individuality in this field is absolute. There are, therefore, no two preachers exactly alike. And no preaching school must attempt to make them alike. That is to say, there is no standard pattern, model, or style to which preachers must be made to conform. There is not even a model sermon. The purpose of a preaching school is to draw out of each preacher his own individual potentiality. It is to make him what he only can be. It is to develop him along his own line. It is to recognize what his form is, his peculiar form, and encourage him to accept it and strengthen it. John Henry Newman was right with his form of preaching because it was John Henry Newman in the pulpit. Dwight L. Moody was equally right with his form of preaching, although it was utterly different from

Newman's, because it was Dwight L. Moody in the pulpit. And both John Henry Newman and Dwight L. Moody might well be too much for King Street Methodist Church or St Agatha's, Little Markettown, where the need is probably for some simple, homely preacher, who by his simplicity and homeliness draws his hearers to the faith in God which he exemplifies and proclaims.

From this it follows that *the ground of a preacher's authority is personal.* He has no authority if trying to be someone else. He has no authority trying to follow a pattern, nor in working from a mould into which he has been thrust or enticed. Neither has he authority if he withholds his individual personality from his preaching. This is in fact only another way of attempting to preach from a mould. No one attempts this in ordinary person-to-person conversation. Something is wrong if a man is 'one thing' in the pulpit and 'another thing' in general life. He is clearly not 'being himself' in both places, and the likelihood is that the place where he is not himself is the pulpit. He is playing a part there. He is an actor, probably a dull actor, but an actor all the same. Then preaching lacks authority. It may be interesting, even astonishing, but it will lack authority. Authority is present only when a preacher is himself. Thus the first work for any preaching school is to free preachers to be themselves. The root trouble with much modern preaching is personal inhibition, producing a lack of animation, of authority, and of power. Freeing the person does not render discipline unnecessary. On the contrary, the more the flood-gates of personality are opened, the more control is required. Power let loose can bring destruction. In preaching, ceaseless attention must be given to word patterns, sentence structure, sermon shape and aim, no less than to delivery, enunciation, emphasis, and speed; but not until the personality of the preacher has been liberated, not until he has accepted that God has made him what he is; not until he has recognized that in the economy of God, the Spirit of God can only use him as he is, for the Spirit of God is the Spirit of Truth and cannot operate through shams or mimicry. The

53

preacher must first be open to God. Only so is the real man discovered to himself. That man he must be when he preaches. Only
so is authority possible, for whatever authority may be granted
by ecclesiastical ordination and/or licence to preach, whatever
authority may lie in expertise, whatever authority is derived from
the message which is proclaimed – and these authorities are real
– the effective authority, the authority which produces power,
is much more subtle; it is personal, it lies in the person of the
preacher and the life in the Spirit which the preacher leads.

To this aspect of authority we are introduced very early in
St Mark's account of Jesus' preaching. Scarcely had Jesus begun
in the Capernaum synagogue than 'The people were astounded
at his teaching, for, unlike the doctors of the law, he taught with
a note of authority' (Mark 1:22; *N.E.B.*). The reason, as we
have already noted[1] was that Jesus did not seek authority by
quoting 'authorities', but by speaking out of his immediate
experience of God. It came through baptism and anointing with
the Spirit; it also came through the thrusting away into the wilder-
ness of temptation by the Spirit. Jesus proceeded to the Capernaum pulpit by way of these personal experiences, and if, as
seems likely, St Mark Chapter One presents us with a typical
day in Jesus' Galilean ministry, he punctuated his continual
preaching with departures to a lonely place for private, personal
prayer (Mark 1:35, 38). It is *this* Jesus who has authority. It
comes from what he is in relation to God.

Authority which resides in the personal is dangerous. The
powers of evil play upon it. Jesus was tempted to use this authority for wrong ends. The preacher, unlike Jesus, may not resist
this temptation. The history of the Christian Church is strewn
with examples of this kind of failure, but if the preacher seeks
to avoid the temptation by denying that the preacher's authority
really is rooted in the personal, he will exercise no power as a
preacher. The pattern is clear in St Mark Chapter One. There is
authority in Jesus' person. There follows power in his preaching,
and this is evidenced by what happens to the hearers.

[1] *Supra*, p. 49.

A further consequence of preaching being essentially a personal activity is that *content and form thus have a focus of unity*. Augustine of Hippo, a preacher of the very first rank, made this discovery for himself. He found that if he was moved by what he wished to say (that is, by the content) when he began to speak, the intensity of his manner (that is, his form of utterance) produced an impact which was immediate. It was the content passing through his person that produced a form effective in communication. The form was not something which a connoisseur might take to pieces; there was no chance of perceiving that the style was a harmonious assemblage of prefabricated parts. A hearer could not be told what exactly he should admire. The entire content and form were inseparably welded in the authoritative and dynamic person of the preacher, so that what was to be admired was immediately sensed, and if not, no amount of 'pointing out' would uncover it. Peter Brown says that 'if we read in the *Confessions* some passage of full-blooded lyricism and compare it with the stilted language in which the same ideas are expressed in one of Augustine's more "classical" philosophical dialogues, we can immediately see that the Latin language has been fused, has caught alight in the almost daily flame of Augustine's sermons.'[1] Augustine's speech as the rhetoric professor was very different from his speech as the preacher. Effective preaching does not come about by the application of the principle of rhetoric to Christian doctrine. The only outcome is an unarresting patchwork in which there is neither unity of theme nor purpose. The Hebrew prophets, so beloved of Augustine, point the way: such a personal awareness of a personal God that to tell of him results in speech patterns that charm and sting the ears. Only so is the knowledge of a God, who is mystery, communicated, namely through fusion of form and content in the medium of personal utterance. Such is preaching.

One final point with reference to the personal element in preaching. It concerns words. Words are not *mere* words in the biblical way of understanding them. *Words are extensions of*

[1] *Augustine of Hippo*; Faber and Faber, 1967, pp. 256, 257.

persons. When God speaks he is going forth in action. Thus God creates with a word, and Jesus heals with a word. And words are not only the instruments of doing, they are the means of being. As Heidegger says, 'Language is the voice of authentic being.' This means that because preaching is an activity with words, it is an activity which is essentially personal. The words the preacher uses are the man, that is to say, they are extensions of him, and according as he is effective or ineffective, so are his words, so is his utterance, so is his preaching.

Our first answer, then, to the question, 'What is the form that is proper to preaching?' is that preaching is proclamation *through a person*.

We turn now to a *second answer*. It is that the form proper to preaching is *poetic*. The way the first answer developed has, in fact, led up to this second answer through the notice that was taken of Augustine's preaching, and the lyricism of the Hebrew prophetic utterance.

God is not a thing. God is not something which can be caught in a net, extracted, examined, measured, weighed, and analysed into its component parts. The scientific approach does not, therefore, obtain in this field of study. God is at least personal, and has all the mystery of the personal and more. And wherever description or interpretation of existence from the angle of the personal is undertaken, a form of expression has to be adopted which brings the reality it touches closer by means of feeling, using word pictures, metaphors, similes and imperfect analogies. This is the method the poet uses when he tries to capture impressions of such basic human experiences as love, desertion, joy, death, birth and exile, vicissitudes out of which the stuff of mortal existence is made.[1] There can only be communication from one to another in words about all these by means of the poetic form of description, not the scientific; and because

[1] No one has achieved a greater mastery in this than the German poet Heinrich Heine (1797–1856).

preaching handles the great themes of human existence in relation to God, it also has to make use of the poetic form if it is really to communicate what can in the nature of things only be known existentially. It is not for nothing that the writings of the Hebrew prophets are largely in metrical form. And it was not for nothing that according to the Fourth Gospel the disciples of Jesus were exasperated by the way he spoke, till one day when he seemed to break away from his normal method they cried, 'Why, this is plain speaking; this is no figure of speech' (John 16:29; *N.E.B.*). The facts are that Jesus was a master of the figure of speech, the parable and the metaphor. In the words of Professor Bowman, he 'was a poet of no mean ability. . . . Aramaic *poetry* was characterized by rhyme, rhythm, parallelism of verse structure. . . . Much of Jesus' teaching was cast in the moulds of Aramaic poetry.'[1] All those who are greatest in communicating in speech the things concerning God use a poetic form of utterance.

Curiously enough, or perhaps it is not so curious, this poetic form grows over the years by a natural process if the preacher really is sensitive to the mystery of the Divine Being and the mystery of human life. It is unlikely that the Hebrew prophets consciously worked at the poetic form of their utterances. What happened is that they themselves became lyrical in speaking about God and his people, and so their utterances became lyrical. Maybe they were subsequently polished, maybe in process of time more conscious art crept into their structure. Such is to be expected, but the impulse and the impetus is not a self-conscious art; the urge to the poetic form springs from the nature of that concerning which the preacher makes his proclamation. A man is unlikely to speak lyrically about the equation:

$$a^2 - b^2 = (a + b)(a - b)$$

The possibilities are very real, however, in describing Israel's

[1] J. W. Bowman in *Peake's Commentary*, Nelson, 1962, p. 738, quoting the findings of Professor Matthew Black. See also the two volumes of *Poems of Jesus*, Robert Petitpierre; Faith Press, 1966.

delivery from oppression in Egypt. Something like Psalm 114 is then probable:

> When Israel came out of Egypt:
> And the house of Jacob from among the strange people,
> Judah was his sanctuary:
> And Israel his dominion.
> The sea saw that, and fled:
> Jordan was driven back.
> The mountains skipped like rams:
> And the little hills like young sheep.
>
> (B.C.P.)

It must be noted also that the Hebrew way of thinking and the Hebrew language were peculiarly adapted for poetic expression. There is a paucity of adjectives and a wealth of concrete nouns. There is also an almost complete absence of the abstract form of expression, and a recurrent use of simple sentences joined together by the copula. Is it for nothing that this mode of picture thinking and this concrete form of language which characterize the Hebrew should be the instruments for communicating the knowledge of God? Is there not an indication here concerning what should be the shape or form of preaching?

This analogy between Preacher and Poet is well drawn out by R. E. C. Browne in his book *The Ministry of the Word.*[1] He writes:

> In a sense the sermon does not matter, what matters is what the preacher cannot say because the ineffable remains the ineffable, and all that can be done is to make gestures towards it with the finest words that can be used. David danced before the Lord, and Michal despised him in her heart for his abandon. The preacher's use of words is his dance before the Lord; the thoughtless may consider his abandon is undisciplined, but his abandon is the fruit of habitual discipline begun in faith and continued in the reason that faith nourishes and by which he protects himself from folly and falsehood. He must study words and forms, he must consider the image and rhythm in case he should say what he

[1] S.C.M. Press, 1958, pp. 15–23.

58

neither means nor wishes to say. Much of his work is like that of the poet, and like the poet he only achieves spontaneity after much labour; not that labour is the cause of spontaneity, but it makes the condition in which spontaneity can be given him. Poets and preachers are moved whenever they remember that forms of words are expressions of the ceaseless creative activity of God without whom no words can be made and used in meaningful conjunction. When a preacher releases his fellows from sightlessness and narrowness he is making a practical expression of his love of God and of his fellows which art makes possible.

In the light of this some advice by Ezra Pound about the use of words is important:

> The more concretely and vividly we express the interaction of things the better the poetry. . . . We cannot exhibit the wealth of nature by mere summation, by piling of sentences. Poetic thought works by suggestion, crowding maximum meaning into the single phrase, pregnant, charged and luminous from within. . . . There must be no book words, no periphrases, no inversions. . . . There must be no interjections. No flying off to nothing. There must be no clichés, set phrases, stereotyped journalese. . . . Language is made of concrete things. General expression, non-concrete terms are a laziness; they are not, not creation. . . . The only adjective that is worth using is the adjective that is essential to the sense of the passage, and not a decorative frill adjective. Every literary sin, every book word fritters a scrap of the hearer's patience, a scrap of his sense of your sincerity.[1]

The preacher who goes to his work in the belief that the sermon is analogous to the poem will not produce a simple result. His sermons may be short, the sentences will certainly be straightforward and the words plain, but the meaning will not lie on the surface. It cannot do if the sermon is about God. As Paul Scherer has pointed out,[2] there is not enough agnosticism in

[1] Letters quoted by Herbert Read, *The True Voice of Feeling*; Faber and Faber, 1953.

[2] *The Word God Sent*; Hodder and Stoughton, 1966.

many sermons to make it evident that they are about the real God. Whatever may be the nature of God and modern man's ignorance of him, man has always at least known that God cannot be as simple as would seem to be the case judged by many sermons. The purpose of preaching is not to make God wholly intelligible. This is impossible. The purpose is to make his presence felt, so that decisions are made in life with respect to the fact of God's existence and his love. The form which preaching takes, therefore, is all-important. It must be the poetic form, with a careful use of words, rhythm, metaphor, and simile. In this Jesus was the Master. He was understood, not understood, and misunderstood, sometimes by the same hearers. Such is the outcome of utterance in the poetic form. Such is the outcome of all utterance about God. If it is disturbing it will be utterance about the real God. It was of the real God Herod heard when the news was brought to him of Jesus' birth. The result was inevitable: 'And when Herod the king heard it, he was troubled, and all Jerusalem with him' (Matthew 2:3). Healing can only follow disturbance. Easter did not take place to comfort us with the news that we are immortal. It disturbs us to seek the life which is offered as a gift. Preaching does not get into its stride till it can disturb and bring the Divine close simultaneously. For this it requires the poetic form.

The form of preaching, we have said, is personal and poetic. Thirdly we assert that it is also *pastoral*. This safeguards the point that the purpose of preaching stretches beyond itself. In preaching, the message is proclaimed through a person, but it is proclaimed in that way in order to shepherd people. In preaching, the message is cast into a poetic form because it is about God who cannot be caught within a net of precise description; but the aim of this poetic form is so that the hearers shall react to the real God who disturbs and heals. The end-point in preaching is never the personality of the preacher, nor the sermon which he delivered, be it never so perfect as an art-form; the purpose is to make men whole. Preaching, therefore, is part of

the pastoral office.[1] It is one of the ways by which the pastor
seeks those who stand in human need. The form of preaching,
therefore, is compassionate, serious,[2] urgent, and with an eye
on response and decision. A sermon is meant to result in action;
first, action towards God, then action towards one's fellow-
men. Preaching is never preaching in a vacuum. It is proclaiming
God to men and women of flesh and blood in a 'life situation',
as the Germans express it.[3] Preaching, therefore, calls for knowledge of people. It calls for knowledge of the contemporary
world and the social situation. Preaching is always dated. If it is
good preaching it is quickly outdated as regards its form. The
content is eternal because it concerns God, but the form is
temporal, contemporary, and temporary. We can prove that
for ourselves by consulting one of the sermons of a master-
preacher of a bygone age. We find ourselves wondering how the
hearers 'sat it out'. The truth is, the form of preaching has to
change because preaching is a pastoral activity. Men change, and
so the ways of shepherding them must change. New patterns of
preaching will, therefore, be necessary,[4] a statement which must
lead finally to a consideration of the future of preaching.

Preaching by word is not the only form the proclamation of
the Gospel takes. Ordination commits a man to the ministry of

[1] See my *A Pastoral Preacher's Notebook*; Hodder and Stoughton, 1965,
pp. 13–25.

[2] Dr J. I. Packer, in describing Puritan preaching, has written, 'The early
seventeenth century was the great age of *witty* preaching. Learned pul-
piteers vied with each other in stuffing their sermons with what Thomas
Goodwin called "the eminentest farrago of all sorts of flowers of wit that
are found in any of the fathers, poets, histories, similitudes, or whatever
has the elegance of wit in it". Preaching thus developed into a sophisticated
entertainment for the cultural, and an occasion for the preacher's self-
display.' *The Johnian* (Magazine of the London College of Divinity),
1957.

[3] *Sitz im Leben*.

[4] For a modern attempt to evolve new patterns of preaching adapted to
hearers unaccustomed to respond to an academic approach see *The
Christian Materialist* by M. E. Dahl; Colin Smythe Limited, 1968. There
is a significant foreword by the Bishop of Willesden.

the Word and sacraments. In the matter of proclamation, sacraments are, in fact, the norm. They are regulative. The charge that could be brought against much ministry of the Word is that it is not in alignment with the sacraments. It does not proclaim God's action in Christ as do the sacraments. It does not envisage regeneration and a new life. It does not make central the broken body and the blood outpoured of Christ. If the sacraments are to be ministered at all they *must* minister these things, they can neither be reduced nor adjusted. What they say, they say. The sacraments, therefore, are the proclamation without which the Church has nothing to say. What preaching should be is a re-presentation of the message of the sacraments, a commentary, an elaboration, an application, a contemporizing of what paradoxically is both historical and eternal.

'The congregation of faithful men'[1] in the locality and in the world at large, also proclaims the Gospel by its existence. In it 'the pure word of God is preached, and the sacraments are duly administered', but by its very existence it says something to the world in which it is set. It says a very great deal when in servant-like fashion it ministers by practical action to the needy of the community. And then the building where the community assembles for worship, inspiration, and fellowship becomes a visible sign of invisible grace available for people. These together with the Bible are time-honoured means of proclamation, by no means outdated in the contemporary world.

New ways, however, are also called for if people are to hear the proclamation. The paperback, the film, and drama have an increasingly important part to play. And more and more the discussion group, the dialogue sermon, and the study session, especially where Church congregations are small, will come into their own. These methods, useful and necessary as they are, must nevertheless be kept under constant review to ensure that they do partake of proclamation. If the foregoing analysis of the form of preaching is at all correct, these other approaches cannot be substitutes for the sermon, but may be extensions of it in

[1] *Art.* XIX, B.C.P.

places and ways suitable for the local needs. We can find instances of this in the New Testament: Stephen disputed (*N.E.B.:* argued; Greek: συνζητέω, discussed) with certain synagogue Jews at Jerusalem (Acts 6:9). Paul also reasoned (*N.E.B.:* argued; Greek: διαλέγομαι conducted a dialogue) in the synagogue at Thessalonica (Acts 17:2), at Athens (Acts 17:17), at Corinth (Acts 18:4), in the school of Tyrannus at Ephesus (Acts 19:9), and in an upper room at Troas (Acts 20:7). The first requirement is to understand what preaching is, then its adaptation to local and contemporary needs will be safe. This subject, however, must be left to a future chapter as must also the question as to where preaching is to take place.

5. The Place of Preaching

WE have inquired into what preaching is. We now turn our attention to the place where the act of preaching is carried out. In other words, where should the sermon be delivered? In church, or in the market-place? As part of worship, or in the discussion group? We can extend these questions. Is the pulpit in church justifiable any longer? Does it need the support of other means of communication, or do other means of communication need its support? What importance can we attach to the *church* sermon?

We begin by observing six major stages in the history of preaching.

First, there is the situation outlined in the book of the Acts of the Apostles. There the Spirit-urged Apostles proclaimed the Gospel of the resurrection of Jesus to a public outside the context of worship. Obviously this extra-ecclesiastical proclamation was the earliest practice with regard to preaching. It is a mistake, however, to infer that the approach proper to every situation, and especially the present, is preaching in the market-place and street corner (or their modern equivalents, microphone or television camera), and to assert that this is where the pulpit properly and normally belongs. On the contrary, we should be careful to note that when Paul proceeded on his missionary journeys in the semi-pagan Graeco–Roman world, it was to the

F   65

synagogues that he made his way in order to preach. This had
been the practice of Jesus. St Mark writes: 'So all through Galilee
he went preaching in the synagogues . . .' (Mark 1:39) Jesus
became, of course, an open-air preacher, but only after rejection
in the synagogues. And when he visited Jerusalem at the last,
it was in the Temple he preached. Indeed, he scarcely seems to
have left it. To teach there was the climax of his ministry. Both
Jesus and St Paul, then, sought out as the place for preaching
the assembly or fellowship of faith. This is because preaching is
essentially speech from faith to faith. It needs that context.
When, therefore, we see St Peter apparently preaching to the
public on the day of Pentecost, we shall be wise to note what kind
of public it was. Not, indeed, a public at worship, but certainly
a public assembled at the Holy City in order to keep a religious
festival. Peter was, in fact, preaching in a community of faith.
And this was the norm in the apostolic preaching. This norm
did not constitute the whole of preaching. Far from it; but
whatever extensions there were, and there were many, in the
interests of mission, the community of faith was the place where
preaching was carried out: the Word was ministered *in the
congregation.*

Secondly, we turn to the situation in the sub-apostolic period.
To describe this a quotation from Justin's description of Christian worship sent to the Emperor Antoninus Pius (*c.* A.D. 150)
will suffice: 'On the day that is called after the Sun, there is an
assembly of all who live in the Town and in the country around,
and the memoirs of the Apostles and the writings of the Prophets
are read as long as time permits. Then when the reader has
finished, he who presides calls on us and admonishes us in a
sermon to imitate all these beautiful things. Next, we all stand
up together and make common prayer both for ourselves and
for all others everywhere.'[1] It is evident from the description that
the sermon was one of three regular constitutional parts of
worship, to which probably a hymn or a psalm was added, and
that this whole structure was based on the order of worship in

[1] Justin 1 Apol. 67. 3 and 65. 1.

66

the synagogue from which it was derived. Here, then, we see the preaching firmly rooted in worship.

Thirdly and *fourthly*, we observe two developments which took place side by side. On the one hand, from the sixteenth century onwards so little attention was being paid to the ministry of the Word that worshippers at Mass were advised, even by such as Francis de Sales, to occupy themselves with suitable meditations while the priest was mumbling through it; and at the same time, the Protestants were so divorcing preaching from its liturgical setting that it degenerated into the intellectualism of seventeenth-century Lutheran orthodoxy, the moralism of Tillotsonian Anglicanism or the emotionalism of the pietistic preaching of all the Protestant Churches.[1]

Fifthly, we note in most recent times a recovery of the whole ministry of Word and sacraments in both Catholic and Protestant Churches. In her formularies the Church of England recognizes her ministry as one of both Word and sacraments, but this balance has not always been maintained. In recent years there has come about a partial recovery of this wholeness in that the ministry of the Word has struggled for a recognized place in the Parish Communion. Moreover, on the Roman Catholic side, Paulinus Milner writes: 'In the Mass we see how the whole action is a celebration of the Word of God, and the whole of that celebration is sacramental; that the breaking of the bread of the Word naturally leads up to, and is consummated in the breaking of the bread of the Eucharist, which is itself the thankful response of those who have heard God's Word – as St Augustine says, a "verbum visibile".'[2]

Sixthly, we see at the present time a growing impatience with preaching in worship. This is probably due in the main to the fact that congregations are declining, and the Church appears as a marginal organization in modern society. Preaching in such a context is largely irrelevant to the main stream of life, because

[1] See R. H. Fuller, *What is Liturgical Preaching?*; S.C.M. Press, 1957, p. 10.
[2] *The Ministry of the Word*; Burns and Oates, 1967, p. 13.

those whom the Church is seeking to reach are not present in services of public worship. Less and less importance, therefore, can be attached to preaching in the traditional understanding of it, and time is not worth the spending on its requirements; other ways of confrontation with the general mass of men outside the Church must be sought. This implies and derives from a gradual minimizing of the part played by the organized Church in the Christian mission towards society.

In all this that is being considered, the crucial point is the relation of preaching to the Church. It is what continental churchmen of the Reformed tradition would describe as the relation of Preaching and Congregation.[1] It could be formulated as a question. Does the preacher stand, as it were, outside or even apart from the porch of his church and proclaim to the public, or does he stand within the congregation, building up its members in order that they shall make that proclamation with him in the midst? In other words, what part, if any, has the Church or congregation to play in the ministry of the Word?

This is no new question. Sixty years ago it was a live issue. P. T. Forsyth, writing in 1907, declared: 'It is characteristic of much of the Christian activity of the last half-century, that it aims not so much at a Christocracy, where Christ has a household and is Master of it, as at a Christolatry – a mere $\lambda\alpha\tau\rho\epsilon\acute{\iota}\alpha$ of Christ, where he is worshipped mainly through the service of the public.'[2]

Between the wars of the twentieth century, however, there occurred a rediscovery of the doctrine of the Church, so that even a Congregationalist theologian could write: 'Christian experience is always ecclesiastical experience.'[3] There was also a concentration on 'the preaching', the *kerugma*, initiated largely by C. H. Dodd, but it did not develop into a revived concern for the ministry of the Word, and there was no tie-up

---

[1] The title of a significant book by J. J. von Allmen, published by Lutterworth, 1962.

[2] *Positive Preaching and the Modern Mind*, p. 50.

[3] J. S. Whale, *Christian Doctrine*; C.U.P., 1941, p. 128.

made between the Church and preaching. On the whole, although the tradition of preaching survived in the Free Churches, backed by a number of pulpit giants, and the Church of England was not without its 'great' preachers,[1] a progressive uncertainty about preaching became widespread, reflected in the popular idea (encouraged by the church leaders) that worshippers should attend church not for what they could get, but for what they could give. This viewpoint, of course, completely overlooked the fact that they might have nothing to give until they had received, and indicated the latent Pelagianism in the average (English)man's idea of religion.

Since the Second World War, preaching has experienced a further uncertainty through two fresh developments, the first of which is a concentration on Ecumenism. This, according to J. J. von Allmen, is slightly contemptuous of preaching.[2] 'Contemptuous' seems a strong word. The Ecumenical Church is certainly not contemptuous of the *kerugma*. Could it not be that the changed situation in which the Churches find themselves today in Europe understandably places a question mark against the traditional sermon as a *priority*? Priority of concern has, therefore, passed to Church unity, and here the focus of attention has been on the ordained ministry and the sacraments, because it is precisely here that the divisions between Churches are most acutely felt. The net result has, however, been a slackening of concern for preaching, certainly of the traditional church sermon, and perhaps also of preaching in its wider connotation.

The second development is the growing interest during the last decade in the Divine activity, not so much in the Church, as in what has come to be called 'the secular'. One of the results is that in so far as place is given to preaching in this line of thought, it is not so much a proclamation of God's acts for men in Christ's incarnation, cross and resurrection, as an indication of what God is doing in contemporary history. There is, of course, a

[1] See Horton Davies, *Varieties of English Preaching*; S.C.M. Press, 1963.
[2] *Preaching and Congregation*; Lutterworth Press, 1962, p. 64.

proper place for this element in preaching, but to make it central shifts preaching from the balance it had on the lips of the Apostolic Church.

Perhaps a third factor making for hesitation about preaching altogether ought to be added. It is the theological ferment of our time. It is not surprising that a reluctance to proclaim should exist where there is a hesitancy about what can be believed, and how what is believed can best be expressed.

From the fact that these developments have coincided with a decline in church attendance, it could be argued that the uncertainty about preaching in general which they have caused is one contributory reason for that decline. If so, no easy or quick solution is to be expected; there are far too many interlocking questions to allow it.

It will be seen that in general there have been three lines of aberration:

1. To concentrate on the sacraments to the virtual exclusion of preaching.
2. To concentrate on preaching to the virtual exclusion of the sacraments.
3. To assign preaching to the position of an activity apart from the Church, and, therefore, drastically to alter its form to suit its new location.

The primary (though not the exclusive) proper place for preaching is, however, within the liturgical worship of the Church, a worship which finds its focus in the Eucharist, but does not end there. It extends to other acts of common prayer and worship, and has as its purpose the building up of the congregation in order that, with the preacher, it may preach to the world. The first sermon (for good or ill) the world encounters is the Church. No wonder the preacher must first preach to the Church.

All this has been well expressed by P. T. Forsyth: 'True preaching presupposes a Church, and not merely a public. And whenever the Church idea fades into that of a mere religious club or association, you have a decay in preaching. Whenever the people are but a religious lecture society, the pulpit sinks. . . . What Christ founded was not an order of preachers, nor an institution of preaching, but a community, a Church whose first charge His preaching should be. It is Church and preacher together that reach the world.'[1] This represents a high doctrine of Church preaching, but not so that the Church is treated as an 'in-group'. On the contrary, preaching is counted as integral to mission. The preaching takes place in church so that the world which is not in church may hear. The question, of course, is one of method.

All this may be clarified by pointing out that preaching belongs to worship, to the fellowship ($\kappa o \iota \nu \omega \nu \iota a$), and to witness; what is more, it belongs to them in this order of priority.

First, preaching belongs to the act of worshipping God, it belongs to the *cultus*. If the whole duty of the Christian man can be summed up in his duty towards God and his duty towards his neighbour, preaching belongs first to the first part. Preaching is primarily an act of worship. Preaching is glorifying God who, in Christ, came for us men and for our salvation. Preaching is our thanksgiving in words, as the Eucharist is our thanksgiving in actions. Both are primarily essential means of communion with God. What we do with the bread and the wine is an act of worship, the purpose of which is encountering the divine presence. What we do in the pulpit is an act of worship with precisely the same end in view. Both in the Eucharist and in the preaching, the people of God are fed and edified; this does not take place independently of worship, but through worship. It is because we *approach God* that we are strengthened.

On this understanding of preaching the similarity to prayer is, of course, close, but preaching is not identical with prayer. The celebration of the Eucharist is likewise close to prayer, but it is not identical with prayer. Both preaching and the Eucharist are carried out in the atmosphere of prayer. It is their breath of life, but they are not the same as prayer. Preaching and the Eucharist

[1] *Positive Preaching and the Modern Mind*, pp. 58–59.

71

are a showing forth, a declaration, an exposition, a proclamation of the Lord's death and resurrection, understood eschatologically, in the congregation at worship; or as St Paul expressed it: 'For every time you eat this bread and drink the cup, you proclaim the death of the Lord, until he comes' (I Corinthians 11:26; *N.E.B.*). Preaching is a declaration of God's approach to man in Christ, by which man is able to draw near to God. This declaration is made in the spirit of worship, and its purpose is to lead on to prayerful communion.

This kind of declaration in worship, which leads on to prayer, is to be found in the Consecration Prayer in the service of Holy Communion in the Book of Common Prayer. It begins: 'Almighty God, our heavenly Father, who of thy tender mercy didst give thine only Son Jesus Christ to suffer death upon the Cross for our redemption; who made there (by his one oblation of himself once offered) a full, perfect, and sufficient sacrifice, oblation, and satisfaction, for the sins of the whole world; and did institute, and in his holy Gospel command us to continue, a perpetual memory of that his precious death, until his coming again . . .' All this before the prayer actually begins: 'Hear us, O merciful Father, we most humbly beseech thee . . .' The outcome of both the declaration and the prayer is communion. A number of the collects are built up on the same pattern, for example: 'Almighty God, who hast given us thy only begotten Son to take our nature upon him, and as at this time to be born of a pure Virgin: Grant . . .', or, 'Almighty and everlasting God, who dost govern all things in heaven and earth: Mercifully hear the supplications of thy people, and grant . . .' Before the petition there comes the declaration which encourages it, and the whole is carried out in an attitude of expectant worship. This is preaching.

In the light of this, the Book of Common Prayer is logical in only actually requiring a sermon at the service of Holy Communion because there the complete context for preaching is provided – the assembled congregation, worship, prayer and sacramental communion.

It could be said that this is a restricted view of preaching. No doubt such a charge would be legitimate if preaching never extended beyond these bounds. It is important, however, to understand, whatever extensions are made, what is its essential nature. Otherwise, preaching can become different from what it should be and then, failing to be effective, is dismissed as a useless activity. In the present century, we have come perilously close to this false estimate with a consequent decline in worship. For let us be aware of this, that if preaching needs worship as its context, worship needs preaching as its stimulus. In recent years much attention has been given to revising forms of worship. This is right; formless worship is an impossibility. There are proper patterns to be followed,[1] but unless attention is also given to preaching, the worship will flag, and in the end the worshippers fail. Preaching belongs to worship and worship belongs to preaching.[2]

There is one other aspect of preaching as an act of worship which calls for attention. An act of worship calls for sacrifice. It is 'a sacrifice of praise and thanksgiving'. For the preacher first it should be 'a reasonable, holy and lively sacrifice'. The sermon is his offering. Not infrequently, preachers have complained, as the priests accused by Malachi complained of their sacrifices, that there is a great weariness in it, with the result that unworthy offerings were made and the table of the Lord polluted. The pulpit is able to suffer a similar fate. It is incumbent upon the worshipper, however, to bring his best. The preacher is first of all a worshipper, and the sermon is his offering. Unacceptable offerings in Old Israel were an index and ground of the whole people's spiritual malaise; it is a diagnosis the New Israel, the Church, will be tempted to side-step; a temptation maybe it would be wise to resist.

Secondly, preaching not only belongs to worship, it belongs to the fellowship, the κοινωνία. There are at least three reasons

[1] See Thomas H. Keir, *The Word in Worship*, p. 100.
[2] In the Lutheran church tradition there cannot be a service of worship without preaching.

for this. First, the preacher is not the only worshipper. His sermon is not the only 'sacrifice of praise and thanksgiving'. In the fellowship in worship, the sermon preached belongs to all present, because it is part of *their* worship. But they also own it for a second reason. Apart from them there would be no sermon. The ministry of the Word depends upon an assembly. A preacher can no more preach in isolation than a communion is possible when only the priest is present. Both ministries involve sharing and, in the case of preaching, the communication involves hearers. Preaching is a two-way business. Thirdly, a congregation owns the preaching it regularly receives in the limited sense that wherever there is a pastorally-minded and competent preacher, what is offered is preaching adapted to the needs of that particular fellowship. That is to say, the preaching belongs to them. It is *their* preaching. In this way they own it. Of course, for a variety of reasons this ideal is not always achieved; but the failure does not invalidate the truth that for preaching to succeed it must belong to those to whom it is addressed, in the sense of meeting them at this point of their need.

The preacher who understands the part played by the congregation in preaching will not neglect this aspect of his work. Here lies the case for dialogue – not dialogue preaching, a highly specialized activity only very few are advised to attempt – but *dialogue for preaching*. The time-honoured method of carrying this out is pastoral visitation. The late A. E. Richardson, D.D., of the Church Army, a preacher eagerly heard by the simplest congregations, acknowledged as one of his devices the open confession to those he visited that some good point they had made in conversation, or some question they had raised, would be handled in next Sunday's sermon. It invariably ensured their presence. Every preacher who is gladly heard speaks because he has gladly received from those that hear. Preaching is the outcome of a two-way activity; behind it is dialogue. This needs to be fostered, especially in the modern world. Behind the preaching needs to be the discussion group, the question evening,

74

the forum where no questions are barred. So not only will the sermon already preached be analysed, but the shape of the one still to come will be fashioned.

Thirdly, we should note that preaching which belongs to the fellowship is the witness of that fellowship. This is what the fellowship would like to say if it had voice. The background dialogue has at least helped, in that preaching thus becomes the corporate, verbal witness of the local Christian fellowship.[1] Preaching is *its* witness, a situation which has its own story to tell when little attention is paid to the pulpit, either by him who occupies it or the congregation that suffers it.

Preaching viewed as witness prevents preaching from ceasing at the church doors. It links it to mission. Preaching is and always has been the inspiration of mission. When preaching is at a low ebb, mission is at a low ebb. Conversely, when mission is at a low ebb, preaching is at a low ebb. Preaching leads to mission. It leads to it because witness forms part of it. When some natives of Cyprus and Cyrene scattered after the persecution that arose over Stephen and made their way to Antioch, they began to speak ($\dot{\epsilon}\lambda\dot{\alpha}\lambda o\upsilon\nu$) to pagans as well as Jews, preaching ($\epsilon\dot{\upsilon}\alpha\gamma\gamma\epsilon\lambda\iota\zeta\acute{o}\mu\epsilon\nu o\iota$) the Lord Jesus (Acts 11:20; cf.8:4). Their witness became their preaching. When preaching *in the congregation* takes the form of witness, it quickly extends as witness *beyond the congregation*. Evangelism has its roots in preaching conceived as witness. The Apostles after the ascension 'went out to make their proclamation (preaching, $\kappa\acute{\eta}\rho\upsilon\gamma\mu\alpha$) everywhere' (Mark 16:20; *N.E.B.*) because they were witnesses of Jesus and his resurrection. Their preaching was their witness. It was also their evangelism.

In our consideration we have moved from the preacher to the congregation, from the individual's part in proclamation to the part played by the fellowship or congregation. There is one other

[1] Where preaching is only thought of in terms of edification the underlying idea of the Church is of a static and not a dynamic body, a group which *is* rather than a group which *does*.

75

aspect which must be pursued, although already touched upon. The process of communication requires not only a speaker but a hearer. It requires not only a speaker with the skills to speak, but a hearer with the skills to hear. A group of foreigners are unable to receive from a speaker, however competent he may be in oratory. This applies to foreigners not only of nationality, but of culture and thought-forms. Speaker and hearer have to be on 'the same wave-length'.

The question therefore arises: 'How is preaching *to be heard*?' When the preacher has done all he can by way of interpretation of his message so that hearing is possible, something still has to be done about the hearers. This is why preaching in the form of the ministry of the Word has to take place primarily in the setting of the congregation at worship, which for most practical purposes means a building set apart, probably permanently, certainly temporarily. It is here in the congregation and in the church building that the hearers are taught to hear.

In a former age they were taught by Gothic architecture and stained glass. These constituted their manual of instruction. And before we write them off as hindrances to twentieth-century men, we should take account of the appeal of the building of Coventry Cathedral, its tapestry and its windows. The age of the evocative power of symbols has not passed.

There is also the liturgy. The regular recital of liturgical phrases by the congregation is an indispensable part of the ministry of the Word. It enables people to hear by providing sensitive spots in the mind. It is in this context that the learning of catechisms, set prayers, and hymns is of paramount importance. It is almost impossible to over-estimate the part played by hymn singing in the Methodist Church as a means by which the congregation is enabled to hear the preaching. This singing is not conditioning or 'softening-up' the hearers. Such is possible and perhaps even prominent in Revivalist meetings, but the proper function which liturgies and hymns perform is the imbibing by the congregation of the divine language, the

76

language of faith by which they are enabled to hear the preaching.

Worship implies the song. In some communities it implies the dance. 'When Pavlova, asked for the meaning of a certain dance, replied, "Do you think I would have danced it if I could have said it?" she was making a reply that the people of the Old Testament, or those in St Paul's day, would have understood.'[1] These responses, however, of song and dance (and for the most part it will be the song) must serve the liturgy. Such must be the office of music: to serve the liturgy. It does not exist in church for its own sake. It exists to lead the worshippers to the place where they are enabled to hear the Word of God, and it bursts forth in a paean of thanksgiving when that Word has been heard; *Te Deum Laudamus*. None of this means that church music must be only congregational and therefore simple. There is a proper place for canticles and anthems sung by a trained choir, but church choirs and church musicians must re- member that the Church's song exists only because of the Church's Word, and the music's very life consists in serving that Word.

Preaching is also able to be heard when attention is given to Bible reading on the part of the congregation. What is implied here is lectures about the Bible explaining its structure and content, study groups where discussions take place, and the private use of the Bible in devotion as encouraged by the various Bible reading associations. The public ministry of the Word is dependent on the private study of the Word,[2] otherwise the hearers will not hear, communication between preacher and hearer will not take place and, in the end, the preacher will cease to occupy his pulpit.

Preaching, then, belongs to the Church, it belongs to the

[1] Thomas H. Keir, *The Word in Worship*, O.U.P., p. 93.

[2] Canon M. A. C. Warren, D.D., made this point in a sermon preached before the Bible Society in the Church of St Andrew by the Wardrobe on 15th May 1968. It is published in the *Preacher's Quarterly*; Epworth Press, September 1968.

congregation,[1] and without the congregation's co-operation it will fail. This is the overriding fact which determines where the preaching takes place, and what is its basic norm.

[1] The Archbishop of York writes, 'We must be frank and face the fact that many congregations have not begun to grasp the truth of preaching as a function of the worshipping congregation. They have regarded it as something done to them whilst they themselves remain passive. . . . When preaching begins, the Church goes into action.' *Preaching: An essay in co-operation*; S.P.C.K., 1963, p. 4.

6. The Future of Preaching

THIS book began by asking if there is any future for preaching. We saw it ringed round by many obstacles peculiarly the product of the twentieth century, so ringed round that it did not seem possible that preaching could escape the encirclement and enjoy any kind of future. But is this so? The question has every right to be asked when care is taken to observe what is the origin of preaching, how it seems to lie within the divine purpose, being in essence the proclamation of the acts of God. It is not foolish to expect that it has a future, even though the nature of that future cannot be readily determined. The purpose of this chapter is to look a little more closely into the possibilities.

We cannot embark on these considerations without noting two facts about preaching. It is a ministry of the Word of God, and it is also a ministry with words. Because it is a ministry of the Word of God, because, that is to say, it is a ministry of God's continuous activity in life (the 'Word of God' meaning God going forth in action) we must expect it to possess a permanent dynamic; but the preaching must be a real ministry of the Word of God and not merely the words of men.

There is also the fact about words and the human. A man is a talking being. It is speech that distinguishes him from the other animals. Presumably the animals communicate with each other (there is evidence for this) but man needs more than

79

communication, he needs communication *by speech*. Speech, then, is necessary for any life which is truly and fully human.

Speech is also the most *effective* form of communication. The picture, the dance, the performance of instrumental music are also means of communication, but they are assisted by descriptions in words which both make the medium convey a meaning to more people, and sharpen and clarify what that meaning is, or may be. Visual aids, too, despite their increasingly widespread use today, are but *aids* to verbal communication, not replacements. Moreover, when words draw upon the whole range of literary forms such as metaphor, simile, analogy and rhythm, their power to penetrate the minds of others is very great. And when further those resources of language are actually spoken forth as words by a person, there is added all the mysterious dynamic of personality conveyed through the voice, the eye, the hand, and even the posture of the body of the speaker. There is no form of communication to compare in effectiveness with the face-to-face use of the spoken word. When all other means of communication have failed in a break between two people, they must go and talk to each other. If this fails, it is failure indeed.

Speech is also the most *speedy* form of communication. We noted that this is an age of speed. Speed does not militate against the spoken word, but rather undergirds it. Modern scientists have for some time known that they cannot use books to communicate their ideas, because books take so long to produce, and by the time they are published the ideas embodied in them may be superseded. Scientists, therefore, fall back on journals, but even these are so unsatisfactory that facilities for direct speech are being provided by the arrangement of accommodation at scientific centres where research workers are able to gather from different countries and stay for extended periods to talk. There is a very real sense in which, because of the speed of modern life, speech has come into its own as *the* means of communication – although such speed of life also creates the situation in which, unless the hearer is in some way convinced of the value of what is being said, he will spare no time to stop and listen.

Modern advances in the science of telecommunication have also enhanced the use of the spoken word. New techniques in the use of submarine cables and the orbiting of satellites have extended both the volume of spoken words that can be conveyed and the area in which they may be broadcast. At a more modest, but certainly more widespread level, the popular use of the tape-recorder in recent years has caused a far greater reliance than formerly to be cast on the spoken word. The up-to-date reporter does not carry pencil and paper, he speaks words into an 'electronic notebook'. Because of this greater need for facility in speech, courses in speech production for business executives are available at quite expensive rates.

In the light of this modern extended reliance on the use of the spoken word, it does not seem reasonable to suppose that the spoken word would have less and less part to play in the com-munication of the Christian message, more especially when what the Church is reckoned to possess is a Ministry of the Word. It is not its use of the spoken word as such that brings into question the value of the sermon today. The problem is rather of the over-abundance of words in modern life; of man's con-sequent death to words; and of the pace of life which militates against any tendency to sit and listen. For the sermon to survive in such a context, its content, form, and delivery must be such that, despite these factors, it will stand out as something worth hearing. It could therefore be that the Church is being driven, or called, which ever way we view the matter, to achieve a fresh skill in the use of the spoken word in order to match the times in which we live. It could be that the twentieth-century Church, lamenting its all too obvious marginal status in society, needs to rediscover and accept its own peculiar status. Too long it has hankered after its bygone general acceptance as a welfare officer or club provider. It needs to shed a 'hybrid' professional-ism and be what it is; not least, a Minister of the Word, openly choosing a ministry which involves words, spoken words. Professor G. R. Dunstan, writing in *Theology*, advised the Christian ministry to seek once more to become a 'learned profession'.[1] What is needed is specialists in divine knowledge. That is to say, the ministry needs to know in the broadest sense what is the Word of God, and if to know it, surely to be able to communicate it; which includes what modern scientists have not found dispensable – communication by the spoken word. The Church which poses as an amateur psychiatrist or amateur welfare worker is bound to be superseded by the State-supported expert. The ministry of the Word is the Church's peculiar work, which in part gives her ministers their proper profession.

This does not mean that preaching will continue to adhere to the old patterns. Nor does it mean that preaching in the accepted sense of the sermon in church worship is the only way in which the ministry of the Word is carried out. There must be new patterns and new approaches to suit the new age in which we live, with its new needs. To live means to change. To resist change means to die. The change, however, should be by trans- formation and adaptation, as a plant changes in different climates or soils, not by sudden and dramatic removal and substitution as in the artificial set-up of the theatrical stage. First, however, we must turn to a consideration of different types of sermon that are serviceable today.

1. The traditional sermon

At the outset there is *the traditional sermon preached in the course of public worship*. There is still room for this. If a total audience of hundreds of thousands assembles in all the churches in Britain on any Sunday morning and words are expected to be spoken, it is plainly fatuous not to cultivate the greatest possible expertise in order that the greatest possible profit may result from the exercise.

What this means in practice is that there is still room, within the traditional context of public worship, for the sermon *which does not expect either discussion or questioning to follow*. The

[1] October 1967. See also S. Neill, *The Church and Christian Union*; Oxford University Press, 1968, p. 277.

sermon preached at a celebration of the Eucharist is a preparation for communion with the Divine Presence, not an introduction to congregational discussion or argument. Nor is Eucharistic worship the only context for the kind of sermon which ushers the hearers into the Real Presence. It can take place at Matins or Evensong, or the morning worship of the Methodist Church. It could be argued that any sermon which does not introduce the hearers into the Divine Presence, where men are silent and the only first possible reaction is prayer, is defective às a sermon, whatever else it may be. The present writer carries in his mind the memory of the impression produced by a sermon preached fairly recently at a large, high-powered ecclesiastical conference gathered for the express purpose of discussion. After the sermon no one spoke. No one discussed the sermon. No one would allow it to be discussed. Somehow we had been taken where all speech is banal. The experience defies description.

The point we are making is that the traditional form of preaching in worship is not the only form, but if it is summarily dismissed as outmoded the judgement is superficial. It is probable, if not certain, that the highest levels of preaching are only possible in the presence of the genuinely worshipping and seeking congregation. It is true, of course, that only rarely does preaching rise to such heights of excellence, due no doubt to defects in both preacher and worshippers, but we should maintain the tradition of church preaching so that the possibility of great preaching may not be lost.

Albert van den Heuvel has something to say on this worth quoting *in extenso*. After describing the need to scrap our neat recipes for sermon construction and to embark on experimental styles, he writes:

> Finally, since we prepare our sermons together in this age, we have given up the great eloquent, rhetorical address. But since our God has a terrifying sense of humour, once in a while he calls a man to behave in a very unchurchly way, and to become a lonely, superb preacher. He is not in any sense the example on which we all have to model ourselves. He is an extraordinary gift

to the Church. God has produced them in Great Britain in quite some numbers. In our day, perhaps, none is greater than the American with the historical name, Martin Luther King.

We all preach our fumbling little sermonettes, so that a tradition may be safeguarded which offers platforms and pulpits to these men. What we perform inside, they shout from the roof-tops. They are the signs of God's incredible patience with us. And they make the impossible ministry worth while.[1]

Preaching of this kind is an art form. This is true even if the sermons it produces today are short and exhibit the grace of simplicity; works of great art frequently exhibit these character-istics. In such sermons there will be an underlying perfection of balance which does not protrude, a careful use of poetic expres-sion, a subtle handling of the treasures of the English language, and such a placing of impressionist illustrations as will illuminate what might otherwise remain beyond the admiration, and there-fore the grasp, of the common man. These sermons belong to the classics of the pulpit. They are the counterparts of Shakespeare and Bach in literature and music. Names like Chrysostom, Augustine of Hippo, John Donne, and Boyd Carpenter enter the mind. Classics are not suitable for every occasion. We do not read Milton in the train, nor use Meissen porcelain on the kitchen breakfast table. But there is an abiding place for classics, which is why they are classics. They do not belong to the prevail-ing fashion which is passing, but to that which expresses permanent insight into the very nature of things.

There can be little doubt that where a settled pastoral ministry exists a large proportion of the traditional form of preaching, that is sermons preached in the course of a service of worship, will have as their aim the guidance of how the members of the congregation are to live out their lives as practising Christians. In this sense they can be described as teaching sermons, though that term is open to possible misunderstanding. Such sermons are obviously concerned with ethics. Sermons cannot dodge ethics. Ethical questions represent the point at which theology

[1] *The Humiliation of the Church*, p. 75.

comes alive for lay people. But there is a tendency in traditional sermons today for ethics to be neglected, if not studiously avoided. The positions of the eighteenth-century pulpit and the twentieth-century pulpit have almost been reversed. In the eighteenth century sermons were largely ethical discourses with little *kerugma*. In the twentieth century, if not largely *kerugma*, they are certainly weak in ethical direction. What is needed is a recovery of wholeness or wholesomeness. Ethical questions must be handled in preaching, else not even biblical theology will be grounded, but there must also be proclaimed ($\kappa\eta\rho\acute{\upsilon}\sigma\sigma\epsilon\iota\nu$) the grace of God which is available in Christ to meet the ethical demand. This means that in all preaching there must be teaching, and in all teaching, preaching (proclamation).

In addition to wholeness there must also be an understanding of how ethical questions should *not* be handled in the pulpit. Only rarely will it be right for the preacher to give specific directions from the pulpit about how Christians should act. Such a situation might be when the whole Church is being persecuted by the State. Then instructions to resist and how to resist might be in place. Generally speaking, however, it will be wrong for a preacher to pronounce in this fashion. It will be wrong, for example, for him to pronounce on medical questions, for he will lack the technical expertise; and on political questions, for he will not be in possession of all the facts; and on personal problems such as marital matters, for he will not know the details of the special situation, and every situation is special. The preacher's task is to set forth the *principles* of ethical conduct, as does the Sermon on the Mount in the New Testament. For example, the preacher is to proclaim that Christians should do in every situation what love demands. He should also give examples of how those principles have actually worked out in certain instances. Such examples have the capacity to become points of revelation to the hearers by which they can discern how they ought to act in their own peculiar ethical situations. What preaching does is to *contribute to the climate* in which ethical decisions can be made in the light of

Christian moral principles. Thus preaching is at one remove from the situation in which the ethical decisions have to be made. And because of this there needs to exist in the congregation a discussion group where the problems can be hammered out, or the confessional, or the interview with 'some learned and discreet minister', or all three. And the existence of these facilities needs to be proclaimed in the preaching. It is here that we arrive clearly at a point where preaching by itself is seen to be inadequate as a means even to guide aright the members of an established congregation. There must be supplementation. People must have situational ethical guidance as well as pulpit proclamation.[1]

2. *The expository sermon*

The *expository sermon* represents a form of preaching at once the most comprehensive and adaptable. This is so because the Bible, being itself proclamation, is both comprehensive and adaptable. It is comprehensive because it uses history, prophecy, poetry, wisdom, literature, the New Testament letters, and much besides to achieve its purpose. It is comprehensive because the Bible is an intrinsically human book. All kinds of men are laid bare in it, and all kinds of motives. There is drama and drabness, pathos and pedantry. The Bible covers life and is therefore capable of providing the raw material of preaching which is contemporary. Moreover, in a picture-conscious age it offers a kaleidoscope of descriptive 'line-drawings'[2] crying out for reproduction by the spoken word. The Bible is an enfleshed presentation of the Word of God ready for the preacher whose ministry is with lips of flesh and blood. But expository preaching must come by way of exegesis. There can be no avoidance of the labour to discover what the Scripture means in its historical setting. Expository preaching, we said, is adaptable. It is

[1] For a number of points in the last two paragraphs I am particularly indebted to Professor C. F. D. Moule, D.D., and his lecture on 'Preaching and Ethics' at the College of Preachers on 11th July 1968.

[2] See R. Rendtorff, *Men of the Old Testament*; S.C.M. Press, 1968, p. 9.

adaptable to contemporary life, but the adaptation will be fanciful and unconvincing unless it is based upon, and regulated by, a scholarly approach to the text of Scripture. Expository preaching requires two disciplines. It requires a thorough acquaintance with the biblical documents, using what tools of scholarship are possessed. It requires also the ability to wield that information in the effort to speak to contemporary man. It cannot be taken for granted that contemporary man is interested in the Bible. It is wiser to take for granted that he is probably not interested in the Bible. If expository preaching is understood simply as painstaking, detailed exegesis, by word of mouth, it will be experienced as a blunt tool. If, on the other hand, the preacher can mirror life and then proceed to reflect it from the Bible, the hearer will be prepared to see himself in the picture and be ready for some word of God addressed to his situation from the Scripture. Expository preaching, it must be borne in mind, is still preaching. It offers no short cut to the skills that are required to captivate people's attention. What the Bible does offer is material, graphic, succinct and pregnant, waiting for exposition; and when attention is devoted to the techniques required, it proves itself captivating to the general run of men who think in pictures. Very few great preachers in the history of the Christian Church have not been skilled in this art. The basic requirement is, however, a deep and flexible knowledge of the Bible, coupled with a clear principle of interpretation. Without this, expository preaching (if not preaching altogether) will flag.[1] Furthermore, expository preaching is preaching in which the authority clearly does not belong to the man in the pulpit 'six feet above contradiction'. What the expository preacher is doing is exposing the authority under which he himself stands. It is the kind of preaching suited to the present age, suspicious as it is of all *imposed* authority. The Bible is not imposed. We do not defer to it on the simple and misleading ground 'the Bible says'. The Bible is the Church's authority,

[1] On this subject John Bright's *The Authority of the Old Testament*, S.C.M. Press, 1967, should be read, especially pp. 162 f.

and the preacher's, and the worshipping congregation's authority, because we have agreed to receive it as the primary document which tells us what our faith is. Expository preaching can be described as preaching *par excellence*. It can be adapted for every age and every group of hearers, and it lends itself to both the traditional sermon and the sermon that leads naturally into the discussion group. Expository preaching has a future; so has the pulpit which offers it.

3. The devotional sermon

The *devotional sermon* is perhaps more commonly called the devotional address. (No one would think of speaking of an expository address.) It belongs mainly to the context of the Christian group, usually small, gathered for some devotional exercise, which can be, and often is, the Holy Communion. Usually it consists of some comments on such aspects of the Christian life as, for example, humility, courage, or self-sacrifice. It can be profound; some retreat addresses (frequently devotional in style) have provided rare depths of spiritual insight. The devotional address on the lips of a master in the spiritual life is able to draw those who hear it into a knowledge of God and of self which no other means is able to surpass. Too often, however, it is shallow and too frequent. A few thoughts about the spiritual life strung together and uttered achieve little; and if the sole diet of a Christian community is no more than this, even though the thoughts be attached to the Epistle and Gospel for the Sunday, debility is bound to result.[1] The devotional address must be the product of devotion, genuine, deep, and personal. Furthermore, the words in which it is clothed must be simple, distinguished, and emotive. It must also be delivered in a voice which is both quiet and confident. There is a continual place for this form of preaching, but it should be recognized

[1] 'There is not likely to be much place in future for the brief hortatory sermon; this kind of exhortation seems to have had its day.' Stephen Neill, *The Church and Christian Union*; Oxford University Press, 1968, p. 276.

that it is more likely to deepen the life of the existing church than to draw the non-committed into its fellowship. It should not, therefore, constitute the sole provision for a church. When it does, decline results.

4. *The evangelistic sermon*

A fourth type of preaching may be called *evangelistic*. This is the complete opposite of the devotional address, and what it seeks is the commitment to Christ of the non-committed. Evangelistic preaching may properly be undertaken in a service of worship in church, for to count all worshippers or even church members as committed Christians is unwarranted. In the past the Anglican Evensong or the Free Church evening worship provided a suitable place for the evangelistic sermon. It is one of the problems of the present time, when evening services are losing their hold, that there are fewer opportunities for evangelistic preaching. Evangelistic preaching is essential. It must take place. There is a necessity laid upon the Church to proclaim the good news to those who are without as well as to those who are within. It is not a profound form of preaching. Its aim is to proclaim Christ in ways sufficiently straightforward for even average men to be moved to say 'yes' to its appeal. There is required a wealth of illustration. The purpose of this preaching is not to proclaim conversion. Men may be – we trust, *will* be – converted by evangelistic preaching, yet salvation by conversion is not what is offered, but salvation through Christ. All men called of God to the ministry of Christ are not called to the work of an evangelist, but evangelistic preaching must find a permanent place in the Church's work, and no preaching should be without at least this thread of proclamation.

5. *The prophetic sermon*

Another kind of preaching is that which we may label *prophetic*. It is as old as the Hebrew prophets, and as modern as the advocates of the 'Secular Theology'. It seeks to point out what God is doing in contemporary history. The situation to which such preaching speaks is one of confusion and bewilderment. Present events seem so bewildering, so complex, that men and women see neither pattern nor purpose in them. If the preacher can show, even in a limited way, that both pattern and purpose exist, a response will be evoked. Obvious cases of public be-wilderment are the incidence and tragedies of war, or some catastrophe in the world of nature, bringing a trail of ruin. But other confusions of a different kind arise. They come about through new developments in common life such as heart trans-plantations and the case for abortion or euthanasia. Here ethical questions are involved, and while it is true that preaching is not to be equated with providing ethical advice, it is at the point of ethical problems that concern over ultimate questions is likely to be aroused. It is in ethics that the pull of invisible constraints is very early experienced. Prophecy is a diagnosis of the con-temporary world-scene. It seeks to tell in moral terms what is actually happening, whatever may be the appearances, and in so doing seeks to declare God's action. In such prophecy the element of forecasting the future is small and does not always receive fulfilment, even in the Old Testament. The important proclamation in prophecy is that God is working his purpose out in history, which purpose is a moral one. The discussion group following this kind of preaching can be most salutary.

Canon Warren has made an important point in connection with this type of preaching. In it, he says, 'the preacher is address-ing not the individual, but the group, the nation, society as a whole'. He continues:

> There may be a particular audience, there may be, for instance, an individual King, such as Ahab, but the individual is seen as the symbol of the community. Always behind the prophet's immediate audience there is a much greater one to which he is speaking.
>
> Whereas to proclaim the good news is to invite individuals to meet God, and in that meeting to know salvation and to enter

upon discipleship, to prophesy is to speak to the corporate conscience.

Nor is this only a feature of Old Testament prophesying. Stephen's apology, and Paul's speech on the steps of the tower of Antonia, were appeals to the corporate conscience of a whole nation, they were not appeals for conversion addressed to individuals.

To prophesy, then, is to speak into some particular situation so as to challenge a corporate conscience.[1]

Such a particular situation at the moment is the whole issue of race relations.

6. *The apologetic sermon*

We come now to the *apologetic sermon*. Paul Scherer is suspicious of this. He writes: 'Apologetic sermons seem to me measurably suspect.' His reason is this:

> Apologetic sermons take it for granted that a sound, rational approach will help a man towards faith; and life seems to honor the theory more often in the breach than in the observance. Which is not, of course, to say that faith is irrational: it is to say that strangely enough and frequently enough to be terrifying – Nazism and Communism have borne their witness to it – the springs of action lie not only with, but beyond the reason. It is to say that faith is what someone has called meta-rational; because it has its being in the realm not just of the mind but of persons.[2]

But we have to preach apologetic sermons. We have to preach them in the nineteen-seventies. It is part of the contention for the faith, the kind of struggle to which the Epistle of Jude testifies: '. . . it became urgently necessary to write at once and appeal to you to join the struggle[3] in defence of the faith, the

---

[1] See *The Preacher's Quarterly*; Epworth Press, September 1968, p. 191.

[2] *The Word God Sent*; Hodder and Stoughton, 1966, p. 72.

[3] The word is ἐπαγωνίζομαι. Its only use in the New Testament is in Jude verse 3, translated 'contend' in the *Revised Version*.

faith which God entrusted to his people once and for all'
(*N.E.B.*). Apologetic preaching has its role because of the
dangers of false belief. Scientism and secularism, for example,
are inimical to the Christian faith, and humanistic and existen-
tialist philosophies can be destructive, too, of that with which
the Christian Church is entrusted. Apologetic preaching represents an attempt on the part of the Church to 'give a reason for
the hope' that is in it; it is not an attempt to win an argument.
Apologetics are Christianity defensively stated.[1] They constitute
an exercise in defence against those who make attack with the
intention not of confounding the opponents, but confirming the
believers. And no small part of apologetic preaching will have
the aim of so restating the Christian faith that in the light of
modern ways of thinking (as for example, evolution) Christians
will not lose their hold on the faith. Following this kind of
preaching, the preacher needs to be available for questioning
or challenging. The discussion group in this case will, as it were,
test the defences.

7. *The question sermon*

There is, however, a seventh kind of sermon which does go over
to the offensive which, for convenience, we will label *question
preaching*. It is the sermon which does not answer questions but
aims almost wholly at asking them. In the modern age, when to
question every tradition and authority is counted as the birth-
right of every individual, when 'the system'[2] is suspect and when

[1] The title of a book by Professor A. B. Bruce, published by T. & T.
Clark, 1892.
[2] 'It is difficult to define "the system". "The system" is everything that
holds up progress. It is the failure of our institutions to be sensitive to the
need for change. "The system" is the uncritical application of bureaucracy.
It is "the usual channels of consultation". It is people in key positions who
refuse to listen to the urgent voice of change. It is everybody waiting for
their turn and the person at the front staying there too long. "The system"
is the system is the system. It makes men into mice, old and untried ideas
out of new ideas.' Des Wilson in *The Times*, 7th March 1968.

dogmatism is out of fashion, the socratic approach in preaching, that is, the method of posing questions, may be the only one either to be given a hearing, or to produce any effect at all. This is especially true in the student world. What sermons of this kind accomplish is a form of tunnelling or undermining of the other's supposed secure position. The hearer listening to such preaching discovers that there are questions deeper and more penetrating than his own, and *the preacher* is asking them. He is thus a disturbing preacher. All truly Christian preaching disturbs before it comforts. What this 'question-preaching' calls for on the part of the preacher is an out-thinking of the rationalist position; it requires mental skill and confidence, and it will look for the gains from such preaching, not in the direct response to the sermon, but in the private conversation or interview which may subsequently and spontaneously arise. This preaching breaks down ill-formed resistance. It does little else, but is the indispensable prelude in some places and some times to building up on the basis of faith.

8. *The dialogue sermon*

There is one further kind of preaching that needs to be considered – the *dialogue sermon*. Few preachers have the required personal gifts for this, but the Reverend Joseph McCulloch at St Mary-le-Bow in the city of London is an exception. So also is the Very Reverend Martin Sullivan, Dean of St Paul's. To St Mary-le-Bow congregations of five hundred are attracted every Tuesday in the lunch hour to hear the Rector defending and commending the Christian faith in public dialogue with some (usually well-known) person who may or may not be sympathetic to the Christian faith, and who is prepared forcibly to voice his criticisms. This is valuable work and wherever it can be done it should be done, but the fundamental needs are for a preacher with the necessary skills (perhaps more could be produced by training) and a closely populated urban area. Another specialized type of preaching for which few seem to be gifted is 'Open

Air Preaching'. The Reverend Lord Soper is one of the very few.

Each of these eight types of sermon has its distinctive and proper function in the total ministry of the Word. It is tempting to allot to the highest place that preaching which introduces the hearers into the presence of God where tongues are still; and to allot to the lowest place that preaching of the questioning, apologetic and dialogue type which deliberately provokes discussion and debate. But all types are necessary, all types are complementary.

Similarly, it is tempting to rank at the top level that form of sermon preparation which is carried out in prayerful isolation by the preacher, because in general it is true that inspiration belongs primarily to individual labour. But it is also true that while inspiration does not belong to what might be called the 'committee approach' to religion, a group working together may, through its corporate travail, bring to birth something as wholesome and original as is normally associated with individual and solitary labour.

In addition we have to recognize that finesse of language will probably not be the product of the question and answer technique, but rather the halting sentence with misplaced punctuation and pauses. Words are easily debased to become snappy counters in our modern interviewing methods. At the same time, finesse of language is not the only, nor the final, criterion of serviceableness of a sermon. There are places and times where finesse could be a positive hindrance. That preaching has to use the language forms of the life in which it operates is almost axiomatic; which being the case, since the halting question and answer method is now so common a method in disseminating news on the television and sound radio, to employ it in preaching may bring as many gains as losses in the Church's work of communication.

In reviewing these various types of sermons, what we must be careful to avoid is assessing one type above or below another type in value. All the different types fulfil their role like members of the body, so that 'the eye cannot say to the hand, "I do not need you"' (I Corinthians 12:21). Moreover, all preaching, of whatever type, must constantly keep before it what preaching essentially is, the proclamation of Christ. This remains true even if the preaching provokes discussion, for it provokes it in order that Christ may be proclaimed at some other time or in some other place. We must at least be able to assert that *the end sought* in all preaching is the 'offer of Christ'.

One of the distinctive features of contemporary life is the move towards partnership in common enterprises. Factory workers are given voice in the management, students at a university are consulted concerning the overall policy. In the Churches the promotion of Synodical Government reflects the same tendency and there is also a move towards more congregational participation in acts of worship. It would be surprising, therefore, if preaching altogether escaped this tendency. The probability is that if twentieth-century preaching tries to escape it there will result a decline in influence of the pulpit in the future. We must, therefore, expect changes.

First, we must be prepared to give an encouragement to congregational participation in preparation. This participation can stretch all the way from the congregation simply being invited, or at least encouraged, to suggest subjects for preaching, to an actual week-night meeting to 'talk over' with the preacher his sermon for the following Sunday. In between these two extremes comes the discussion group (out of which the preacher openly chooses his sermon subject, thus attempting to answer actual questions raised) and the question time following the sermon (through means of which the hearers seek to understand more clearly what was in the preacher's mind). Congregational participation in any form is not possible everywhere. It is not easy to envisage its operation in cathedral worship, though successful experiments have been conducted at Coventry. The

95

greater difficulty is to achieve it in rural areas where the wor-shippers are not articulate. Probably the best results are obtained in the suburban parish, especially where there is a high propor-tion of young people. There is no doubt, however, that where congregational participation is possible the ministry of the Word on the part of a preacher of average gifts will be stimulated and enriched.

Secondly, it is probable that where a congregation is very small, say less than twelve persons, some form of discussion or Bible reading with comment is preferable during the normal act of worship, reserving the more formal sermon for festival Sundays or other special occasions. This could result in en-hancing the importance of the sermon and contributing to the conservation of a tradition which might otherwise fade out to the Church's eventual loss.

Thirdly, and developing from the previous point, it is probable that fewer sermons ought to be preached. Undoubt-edly, some clergy preach too frequently, to the detriment of their own souls' (and perhaps bodily) health, and that of their congregation as well. Some clergy ought not to preach at all. There must, however, be a policy about this reduction of sermons. Simply to say 'we will preach fewer sermons' could result in a mere slackening of the pressure on the ministerial life with no benefit to either preacher or people. What is required is more attention to the principle of team work, in vogue in other departments of life today. What is implied is not a team of clergy or ministers working a group of Churches in the sense of each one carrying out a segment of the whole task, but a collegiate ministry where each one performs the ministry which nature and grace makes clear is peculiarly his. One of these ministries is preaching. Not all are called to be preachers, but some are. These should function as members of the body of Christ with no sense of superiority over other ministries, according to the principles enunciated in I Corinthians 12. The preachers should be the spokesmen of the ministerial teams to which they belong. They would not act independently. They would not build up the body for their own sake. They would not work separately from, but closely connected to, a pastoral setting, helping to accomplish the mission of the Church in a particular area. Some such arrangement as this is preferable to the formation of a team of preachers available for visitation to a variety of Churches in a given area, such as a diocese. Preachers must belong to a definite situation. They must belong to a congregation. They must belong to a pulpit.

Preaching is not a separate profession, it is one way in which the pastoral office is accomplished.[1] There ought also to be an alteration of the present position in the Church of England, where ordination to the diaconate is automatically taken to include the licence to preach. Few actions would do more to improve the standard of preaching than the requirement of a licence to preach (which could also be given to laymen). The licence should be contingent upon certain qualifications, both theoretical and practical, and upon attendance at a course of training in preaching. This should certainly be required for those who broadcast. There must surely be something wrong when preachers are chosen for these ministries independently of the bishop.

Fourthly, there need to be recognized courses of training in preaching along the lines organized by the College of Preachers. It is not possible for the whole art and technique of preaching to be taught in a theological college. The primary task of the theological college anyway is to equip its students with theological tools. It is here the *basis* of preaching can be taught in a man's student days, but the *full skill* is only possible when he has tested himself in the pastoral office, and has both discovered what his peculiar calling is (it may not be preaching) and what the requirements of preaching are in general, and for himself in particular. There are no two preachers alike. There is no standard pattern or mould. Each preacher has to be developed

---

[1] The Lutheran Church gives preaching a disproportionate emphasis, so that the Church appears as its creation, the Church is an *Ereignis*, an event. Thus the continuity of the Church as represented in the sacraments is underestimated.

along his own line. This is the reason for courses of instruction and personal guidance available for clergy and ministers who have tested their own strength and weaknesses in attempting to fulfil this pastoral office.

Fifthly, there needs to be a revival of societies for sacred study among the clergy and ministers, preferably on an ecumenical basis with prominence given to corporate Bible study. In these local and regional groups[1] profitable work could also be done through reading aloud the sermons of various masters in the pulpit. It would train in intelligent reading, and it would provide the opportunity to learn how various preachers construct their sermons, and why it is their content is able to be received. There is no doubt that such exercises would result in considerable enrichment of the ministry of the Word today.

The ministry of the Word does not, however, all rest on the occupants of pulpits, *but also on the occupants of pews*. Preaching must be worked at from both ends. A decline in lay Bible reading results in a decline in biblical preaching, and subsequently in preaching altogether. It is important to note that two of the effects of *aggiornamento* in the Church of Rome are preaching *and* Bible reading. The two go together. The work of organizations like the Bible Reading Fellowship and the International Bible Reading Association needs strengthening in British Church life. There is also a need for popular biblical exposition of the lecture type in centres where it can be encouraged. Ways and means must be sought, varying according to the local situation, whereby study of the Christian faith can be encouraged. The method of cells or group meetings in houses is a present-day possibility. The underlying principle in all this is that people must be given ears with which to hear preaching. This is effected to no small extent by engendering interest. People will hear if they wish to hear, and the existence of such

---

[1] Local groups of this kind have been formed in the Newcastle and Southwell dioceses through the energies of local leadership.

a willingness is to no small extent responsible for the preaching that becomes available. In this sphere, as in others, the demand affects the supply.

A note must be added on the *delivery* or *style of sermons*. To forecast the future in this matter is not possible. We should note, however, that the present is different from the past. If a preceding age favoured an oratorical style with sentimental overtones, this is now out of fashion. In the field of public speaking science has had its effect, as in many other fields. Science distrusts emotion. Therefore a modern, scientifically-conditioned public – and this includes the Christian community, for it is not isolated from the age in which it lives – distrusts emotional speaking. It will almost wholly reject utterance which is lacking in hard facts and is weak in logic. It cannot be said that the late William Temple's preaching was outstanding as regards style, or even artistically attractive, neither did he possess a voice comparable to his predecessor Cosmo Gordon Lang; but twentieth-century scientifically-conditioned people, especially the young, heard him gladly, captivated by the sheer force of his learning, logic, and lucidity. Few will be able to emulate William Temple in the massiveness of his learning, but it is more towards his style than towards Cosmo Gordon Lang's that the twentieth-century public requires the modern preacher to veer.

The preacher must, however, be adaptable. He is not asked to preach in a 'dead-pan' voice, supposing that on this account he will be given a hearing. The reverse will be the case. Nothing kills hearing so much as a deadly speaker. The first essential on the part of a speaker is life, dynamism, and personal involvement; but there are times, perhaps many times, in the modern world when these gifts and acquisitions must be directed chiefly into forceful, unemotional and acutely logical utterance. Today there is a need in the pulpit for a touch of the style of the Edwardian advocate Rufus Isaacs. Logic, it is true, cannot carry the whole way in a pulpit because what preachers have to do with is ultimate mystery which requires poetry; but today the element of carefully presented logical argument must be large, and there must be a voice to match the content. Emotion also has its part to play, but it must be kept in strict control.

One of the implications of this modern requirement is that the preacher must be a learned man. This constitutes a call for the re-establishment of the Christian ministry as a learned profession; not that learning of itself will suffice for the pulpit – there needs to be also skill in communication – but the latter cannot survive without the former; men will only listen if they feel that one of their fellows (and we must remember that a clergyman is still that) has something to say. Dean Inge was accounted gloomy and was anything but popular, but people flocked to hear him for the simple reason that they knew he had something to say.

In a letter to *The Times* (30th March 1967) on 'Christian Intellect' Walter James pointed out that 'men catch belief most readily, it seems, from leaders whose minds they recognize as superior to their own, and minds withal that have conquered doubt'. He also showed how the leaders of most successful religious movements and revivals, even the more popular, were men of high intellectual ability, with a high proportion of dons among them. John Wesley, Keble, Pusey, Newman, Maurice, Gore, and William Temple were all dons. Added, however, to their powers of intellect was strong character. Wesley was tough, and his hypnotic eyes could silence an angry mob. Keble was sought out by worried men in his country parsonage, not only because of his 'double first' but because of his serene and invincible faith. Christianity depends very greatly on the intellect, especially in its exercise of mission. Evangelism only succeeds when it is directed by the intellect. When Newman got his Oriel Fellowship they rang all the bells of Trinity, 'and,' says James in his letter, 'well they might'. There can be no doubt that if the pulpit is to be strong in Britain, more graduates will be required in the ranks of the ministry, and care will have to be taken to see that the Church is not trapped into denigrating the importance of academic learning. Attention must also be paid to clarity of expression. On the whole the academic theologians who appear on television with their hesitating inconclusiveness present a sorry sight. This is not the style for twentieth-century preaching.

Two more questions call for attention. First a practical question, and secondly a theological question. First, *the practical question*. It arises out of the dilemma posed by the first chapter of this book. It can be formed as follows. Granted that the proclamation of Christ, apologetics, and witness form an essential function of the life of the Church, is it, however, right to assume that this of itself justifies the traditional sermon as the best means of fulfilling that function today? Or might not the use of some other media be a more effective means of communication?

If this question is asking whether preaching in the form of the traditional sermon ought to be abandoned within the life of the Church as a means – possibly even the chief means – of edifying its members and those who are loosely attached to it, the answer should be no. Preaching represents truth through personality. It represents face-to-face confrontation, not only between men and men, but between God and men. It is an extension of the principle of the incarnation. 'And the Word became flesh and dwelt among us' (John 1:14). It is when we are at worship of the God who in Christ we conceive of as (at least) personal that we are open to the channel which has the possibility of being the richest for divine communication, being pre-eminently personal. Because of this unique potentiality the traditional sermon preached in the course of worship must remain. There is nothing comparable with which to replace it. Nothing we know is deeper, richer, and fuller than the personal.

If, however, the question is asking whether proclamation by the traditional sermon is the *only* means by which the preaching function of the Church can be fulfilled today, the answer must also be an emphatic no. The sermon in worship as a means of communicating the Word of God requires supplementing in many different ways *within* the structured life of the Church.

101

The Eucharist is a standing reminder of this necessity. Ever since the Church began there has been proclamation through art as well as through words, and it is certain that in our day drama, music, exhibitions, pilgrimages, processions, 'walk-ins', and many other activities will be needed, as well as books, magazines, films, discussions, 'teach-ins' and devices not yet known to us in the mid-twentieth century.

And to go even further, if the question is asking whether the traditional sermon in worship is the best means today the Church can devise of proclaiming its message to the world *outside the Churches*, the answer again must be no. The Church's duty of proclamation to the world must be fulfilled by other means. An obvious need is for it to master the technique of the mass media, notably television, and to use the opportunities provided. In spite of the recently-established schools for teaching the clergy and ministers this art, it cannot yet be said to have been mastered.[1] Religious television is not notably successful. And in this field Church services and the televised sermon are not the most effective means of communication, though the strange power of Bible stories retold has been demonstrated.[2] And theological discussion makes its appeal only to a tiny handful of intellectuals, and does not, therefore, seem a proper use of a mass medium of communication. Surely drama[3] – and not necessarily narrowly religious drama – is the best means by which the limited but important task of making goodness interesting and attractive can be carried out. The Church desperately needs today playwrights, poets, novelists, painters, and musicians because it is likely that the arts will prove the most telling media in the mid-twentieth century for communicating the message the Church has to give. Perhaps these media are at best a *preparatio evangelica*. Perhaps the Gospel cannot in the end be comprehended without the use of language which, of course, need not neces-

[1] The use of sound radio for religious proclamation was being mastered just about the time when it was being superseded by television.
[2] By David Kossoff.
[3] See F. W. Dillistone, *Dramas of Salvation*; Bles, 1967, p. 9.

sarily be spoken language. Words seem to be essential in the last resort. But the use of other media is of paramount importance until the time comes for words to be used. It is unlikely, humanly speaking, that the Church will make much impact upon contemporary society unless there are raised up gifted men and women able to communicate through these artistic media by the quality of their work. Four of the most influential writers of the twentieth century, although not Christians, have shown their pre-occupation with questions which, at bottom, are religious: Joyce, Aldous Huxley, D. H. Lawrence, and Camus. This artistic field is the field in which answers must be given, and the media of communication which operate these are essential. Clearly, a new type of missionary for these areas is urgently needed.

We have now reached the point in our consideration of the future of preaching to ask what *theological questions* are most involved if it is to survive. In the last resort, preaching depends on theology. Perhaps it would be more accurate to say that it depends on Christology for, after all, preaching is the proclamation of Christ. Preaching, therefore, is only convincing if Christology is convincing, and Christology cannot be convincing if it is worked out with a world view, a *Weltanschauung*, which no longer exists. This is why the preacher has to take the modern concentration on the secular seriously. He has to appreciate it and see how it has developed on Christian soil.

The basic structure of our christological confession must be 'Very God' and 'Very Man'. This is the offence and foolishness of the Gospel. Today the 'Very Man' is not in doubt, though it is still important for preachers to stress this with illustrations from the Gospels. But to show Jesus as 'Very God' is difficult. The problem is that the word 'God' may not be meaningful as it once was. Modern man is not interested in the metaphysical, only in the functional; the former he is happy to bypass. How then can we take the word 'God' and apply it to Christ? And if we must believe in God before we can believe in Christ, would it not be, as Ebeling has rightly asked, that Christ did not come to the *ungodly*?

Does all this mean that the one and only point *from which* we can arrive at any meaningful interpretation of what 'truly God' means is Jesus as 'Very Man'? But even if this is true, is the step *from* 'Very Man' *to* 'Very God' able to be taken by any steps of logic whatsoever? We talk of inductive reasoning replacing deductive reasoning as being the only acceptable kind, but can reasoning of *any* kind bridge the gap between 'Very *Man*' (which Jesus was), and 'Very *God*' (which is our article of faith)? Is it not true that we cannot bypass or omit faith? And does not this mean that the preacher must present Jesus as 'Very Man' *in the belief that*, as in Galilee and Judea, so through preaching men are brought to a point where they run out of their depth and are forced into the recognition of a Something Beyond? That Jesus, 'the Very Man', has his chief significance *at this point* must be the peculiar and proper faith of the preacher. He proclaims Jesus the Man because somehow in him the Other draws near or, to use an older phrase, 'the Beyond becomes akin'. So Christ is God for us. In him we have met the Transcendent. In him the Transcendent is realized.

It is these questions of Christology and the Transcendent that need to exercise the minds of preachers in the immediate future. What is required is a Christology that is both simple and convincing, for only by its Christology can preaching hope to convey good news, and only by conveying good news can preaching be joyfully delivered and joyfully received. And the Christology must introduce to the Transcendent. Preaching will not survive if it is no more than humanistic lecturing with Christian overtones. There must be a thorough appreciation of the secular, but an appreciation that the secular is not the whole; Christ is the frontier gate to Something Beyond.

Christology and the Transcendent must occupy the forefront of the preacher's mind in the immediate future, and if there are two subjects only slightly less important, they are the need for a natural theology[1] and a careful representation of Christian ethics; and for this reason: that these two subjects are 'ways in' to the mind of modern man. Perhaps *three* points of entry could be listed: Man himself, the natural order, and the problems of right conduct.

How shall the preacher preach today and tomorrow?

With bold speech, but with an acute sense of the difficulty of belief.

With a clear grasp of what is meant by the authority of the Scriptures, his chief stock-in-trade, together with a sympathetic understanding of biblical criticism.

With a marked respect for reason and logic in the manner of his utterance.

With an unselfconscious use of myth and symbol, image and analogy.[2]

With a firm belief in the Holy Spirit as the Divine hermeneut, the interpreter of Christ who is the way to God, the Transcendent, a Trinitarian faith.

Twentieth-century preaching is no doubt encircled with problems, but it will escape to new life with change and transformation.

[1] Dr Cleobury has attempted this in his book *A Return to Natural Theology*; James Clarke, 1967.

[2] Because we have to show what God does and how he is experienced. Language about what God is, is meaningless.

Epilogue: Preaching in Context

PREACHING always needs a context. It cannot stand out of context. It requires the context of the preacher's person, the context of the congregation, and the context of all that is meant by service. Without these it will be misunderstood; it may even be offensive, and certainly in the end it will fail. Preaching is an activity unable to exist in isolation.

Preaching requires the context of the preacher's person. Whether we relish the fact or not, a preacher is heard *in the first place* not because of the content of his message, nor because of its attractive form, but because of the man who is uttering it. Sir Winston Churchill said as much when asked about the secret of successful public speaking. He replied, 'It is not what you say, nor the way you say it, but who you are.' The first requirement for preaching the Christian Gospel in any age is men to embody it. The people of Galilee listened to Jesus because they were impressed by his person. They came to learn how he was what he was, and how he did what he did. The stark truth is that only Christ can truly preach Christ. Only men in whom Christ dwells can make effective Christian proclamation. What a preacher is in himself is the indispensable context of preaching, and what he is in himself does not derive from preaching schools or books of theology, but from his own reactions to the changes and chances of his own mortal life in faith or unfaith.

Preaching also requires the context of the congregation. If the preacher owns and is owned by no congregation his preaching will carry little weight. If the congregation is weak in Christian discipleship, or its administration is faulty, the preacher's preaching will suffer in effectiveness. Strong preaching requires a strong Church order. It also requires a strong congregation, if not in number, certainly in devotion. The congregation, the Church, reinforces or negatives preaching more than it knows; it is preaching's conditioning context.

Preaching also requires the context of service, and at no time more than the present. So true is this that it might almost be excusable to pray for silence from preaching until the Christian Church really showed that, like her Master, she was prepared to stoop to the work of the household slave and wash the disciples' feet. Words are no substitute for works. Neither, however, are works substitutes for words. Jesus healed and Jesus preached. To eschew either is to forfeit balance. We must work the works of Christ while it is day. This is Christian service. It is the context preaching always needs.

Preaching today will not be like the preaching of yesterday or the preaching of tomorrow, but its context is unchanging: preachers in whom Christ dwells, congregations where Christ is manifested, and works of mercy that all the world can recognize as stemming from his message.